MENNONITE MEN CAN COOK, TOO

Celebrating Hospitality with 170 Delicious Recipes

Willard Roth

Good Books

New York, New York

Contents

Eight decades as host and guest at home and away

Lover of parties and people
Thank you for the gift of celebration
And the way your joy has touched us
Through 2000 years of festivals and holy days
Feast days and fast days, dinners and picnics,
Holidays and reunions, weddings and dances,
Birthdays and funerals
Reminding us that serious concerns
Too often divide us,
That love and laughter heal us
And make us one

—Joy Cowley, Aotearoa, New Zealand,
adapted from www.JoyCowley.com

Men and women attracted to Jesus in the early days were common people. They lived ordinary lives, pursued everyday interests, maintained human routines. When Jesus's followers chose to join the disciple community, they didn't suddenly change from human form to holy stature. In most ways they continued to live like their neighbors: sleeping and waking, working and playing, drinking water and eating bread. Luke paints a simple picture of the daily routine after Pentecost. "Day by day, as they spent much time in the temple, they broke bread from house to house and ate their food with glad and generous hearts" (Acts 2:46).

In reviewing my eighty years as part of the global family, I find no better words to sum up the rich goodness of those decades: *sharing food with a glad and generous heart*. Linking the preparing and partaking of food with synonyms like pleased, delighted, happy, joyous, and cheerful alongside bounteous, lavish, and munificent quickly brings back marvelous memories—enough food memories to fill a few books.

Cues from the Cook's Kitchen

Blend color, texture, and taste as you plan.

As a literarily deprived child, I devoured nursery rhymes with special fondness for lean Jack Spratt, tubby Peter the pumpkin eater, Miss Muffet who hated spiders, and the supper soloist Tommy Tucker. Now that I am older I find similar intrigue in recipes, whether old or new.

A yellowed undated *Elkhart Truth* clipping in my files is headlined "Mesopotamian Clay Tablets Hold World's Oldest Existing Recipes." Recipes inscribed on three Mesopotamian clay slabs dating to 1700 BC are probably the oldest cookbooks in existence, according to the curator of Yale University's Babylonian Collection of which the slabs are a part. The tablets provide instructions for dozens of stews, vegetable dishes, and meat pies revealing "a cuisine of striking richness, refinement, sophistication and artistry," a French scholar commented (*Biblical Archaeology Review*, March 1985). The first printed cookbook appeared in an undated edition around 1475 in Paris. The first cookbook published in America was a 1742 reprint of an English tome titled *The Compleat Housewife*. Printed cookbooks continue to be bestsellers in a Kindle age.

In a September 2012 cover feature story, *USA Today* writer Bruce Horovitz anticipates how an American kitchen might look thirty years ahead. Chef Cat Cora, the first woman to be inducted into the American Academy of Chefs Culinary Hall of Fame, projects that every home will have a computerized kitchen where the cook will walk in, talk to the appliance, and it will do whatever asked. Healthy food will dominate: burgers will be super-lean and low in fat with whole-grain buns; fries, often made of sweet potatoes, will be baked; salads will be local and sustainable. "The home-cooked meal will become more commonplace. As technology evolves in the kitchen, at-home cooking also will be easier than ever," Horovitz predicted; "Dinner increasingly will be eaten at home, because it will be so nutritious and simple to prepare."

Thus it would appear that old fashioned home cooking will not go away soon. To keep the tradition going, home cooks do well to take time to plan their endeavors. Planning ahead enables premeditated shopping to maximize dollar value, to balance nutrition, and to enhance sensual appeal—cheap, healthy food no one will eat is not a good plan. I anticipate how colors, textures, and tastes fit together as I plan. If food looks good and smells good I wager it will also taste good.

Along with a seasonal farmers market, I comparison shop two supermarkets, taking advantage of weekly and seasonal specials, coupons, and house labels. I put non-perishables in my cart first, then frozen and dairy items, and finally fresh produce. I plan for double duty: foods that fit two different recipes; double use of oven with two different dishes; double portions for planned-over's the second time around.

I use my culinary common sense in my planning. I plan with flexibility to take advantage of last-minute invitations to be entertained or eat out. My bottom line: what comes from my kitchen must be nutritious, economical, appetizing to the eye, and appealing to the palate.

Eight decades as host and guest at home and away

1933–1942

Elmer and Minnie's first three children were male. In allocating farm chores with fairness, it seemed that at least one should be assisting indoors. Whether as draftee or volunteer I no longer remember, I was Mom's kitchen associate early on. My male mentor was Uncle Vernon, Dad's brother ten years my senior. I admired him in many ways—he seemed more like an older brother than an uncle. Through the years he supplemented his farming occupation with restaurant cooking and baking. Father helped my mother during canning season with special jobs like husking corn and cutting it off the cob, shelling green peas, and peeling peaches. Grandpa Ben Roth did all the family food buying—grocery shopping is naturally in my blood stream.

To round out a non-sexist curriculum senior boys and girls at Iowa Mennonite School switched manual training and home economics for one semester. I was pleased and quickly made the transition to baking bread, but didn't do as well mending socks.

As the first grandson born to firstborns on both sides of the family tree, I was loved and beloved by twenty aunts and uncles during family get-togethers unlimited. By definition, those gatherings centered on food, fresh from Iowa gardens and farms—often in festive mood, always in bounteous supply. The finale was frequently hand-cranked ice cream with many toppings, whether an outdoor picnic in the park or a Sunday dinner on a linen tablecloth. When the party celebrated a birthday there was always angel food cake with precisely counted candles.

STARTERS

APPETIZERS

Pennsylvania Railroad Stuffed Celery

MAKES: 6 servings

PREP. TIME: 15 minutes

CHILLING TIME: 15 minutes

INGREDIENTS:

6 oz. low-fat blue cheese

3 Tbsp. butter, softened

6 ribs celery, washed and trimmed

¼ cup finely chopped almonds

1. In bowl, blend cheese and butter.

2. Fill each celery rib with a generous mound and coat with almonds.

3. Refrigerate at least 1 hour. Cut each rib into 3 or 4 pieces before serving.

Trains have long been my choice for distance travel. In a pre-Amtrak era, dining-car eating capped the experience. To get taste buds salivating, Pennsylvania Railroad's relish plate always had this quality but uses simple staples, easily reproduced and multiplied for at-home entertaining.

Crab Dab on Home-Baked Chips

MAKES: 12 servings (of 4 each)

PREP. TIME: 15 minutes

BAKING TIME: 15 minutes

CHILLING TIME: 4 hours or overnight

Yield not to the temptation of shortcuts, using canned crab or store-bought tortilla chips. Fresh seafood and chips from the cook's oven transform this offering from ordinary to extraordinary.

INGREDIENTS:

¼ cup low-fat cream cheese

¼ cup sliced green onions, with tops

2 Tbsp. light mayonnaise

2 Tbsp. fresh lemon juice

1 tsp. ground cumin

½ tsp. sea salt, *divided*

¼ tsp. freshly ground black pepper

6 oz. fresh crabmeat, strained

½ cup fresh corn kernels, uncooked

6 6 ½" corn tortillas

2 Tbsp. olive or canola oil

48 fresh parsley leaves

1. Combine cream cheese, green onions, mayonnaise, lemon juice, cumin, ¼ tsp. salt, and pepper in small bowl.

2. Stir in crabmeat and corn. Refrigerate up to 24 hours.

3. Stack tortillas and trim edges to 5" square. Brush each side with oil. Restack and cut into 4 squares; halve each square to make triangles.

4. Arrange triangles on baking sheet; season with salt. Bake at 350° until golden brown, about 12 minutes. Cool on sheet. (When cool, may be stored in an airtight container up to 24 hours.)

5. At serving time, top each baked triangle with 1 tsp. of crab mix and garnish with parsley leaf.

Shrimp Ball in Sunflower Seeds

MAKES: 18 servings

PREP. TIME: 15 minutes

CHILLING TIME: 1 hour

INGREDIENTS:

8 oz. low-fat cream cheese

¼ cup finely chopped red onion

½ tsp. garlic powder

½ tsp. freshly ground black pepper

1 tsp. sea salt

1 Tbsp. chopped fresh basil

1 Tbsp. chopped fresh chives

1 Tbsp. ground horseradish

¾ cup frozen baby shrimp, chopped

¾ cup sunflower seeds, roasted

miniature crackers

1. Combine all ingredients except sunflower seeds and mix in bowl.
2. Form into ball and roll in sunflower seeds.
3. Cover and let rest in refrigerator for at least 1 hour.
4. Serve with miniature crackers.

Parmesan-Stuffed Mushrooms

MAKES: 24 servings

PREP. TIME: 15 minutes

BAKING TIME: 20 minutes

INGREDIENTS:

- 1 ½ lbs. fresh mushrooms, medium size
- 8 oz. low-fat cream cheese, softened
- ¾ cup + 2 Tbsp. freshly shredded Parmesan cheese
- ¼ tsp. sea salt
- ¼ tsp. freshly ground black pepper
- ¼ tsp. ground nutmeg
- ½ tsp. Worcestershire sauce

1. Clean mushrooms with paper towel; remove stems. (These may be used in other recipes, at cook's discretion.)
2. Place mushroom caps facing up on greased baking pan.
3. Combine remaining ingredients, except the extra Parmesan, and mix well.
4. Spoon cheese mixture into caps; sprinkle with extra Parmesan.
5. Bake at 350° for 20 minutes. Serve warm.

Salmon Pecan Pâté

MAKES: 24 servings (2 ½ cups)

PREP. TIME: 20 minutes

CHILLING TIME: 1 hour

INGREDIENTS:

- 15-oz. can wild-caught pink salmon, drained, dark skin removed, and flaked
- 1 Tbsp. fresh lemon or lime juice, plus zest
- 8 oz. low-fat cream cheese
- 2 Tbsp. light mayonnaise
- 2 Tbsp. finely chopped onion
- 1 Tbsp. finely chopped fresh parsley
- ¼ tsp. hot pepper sauce
- 2 tsp. Worcestershire sauce
- 1 tsp. freshly ground black pepper
- ½ cup finely chopped pecans
- fresh parsley
- sesame sticks, *or* fresh vegetable sticks

1. Put salmon in bowl, and add lemon juice and zest. Mix in cream cheese, then mayonnaise, onion, parsley, hot pepper sauce, Worcestershire sauce, and black pepper.

2. Cover and refrigerate for at least 1 hour.

3. Dish into serving bowl, top with pecans, and garnish edges with parsley.

4. Serve with sesame sticks or fresh vegetable sticks.

Water Chestnut and Spinach Dip

MAKES: 24 servings

PREP. TIME: 10 minutes

CHILLING TIME: 2 hours or overnight

INGREDIENTS:

16 oz. frozen chopped spinach

8-oz. can water chestnuts, drained and chopped fine

¾ cup light mayonnaise

¾ cup plain Greek yogurt

1-oz. package Knorr's powdered vegetable soup mix*

12-oz package pretzel sticks

*Note: use only this brand to maintain quality

1. Cook spinach 1 minute in microwave and squeeze dry.

2. Mix cooked spinach in bowl with water chestnuts, mayonnaise, Greek yogurt, and soup mix.

3. Cover and refrigerate for several hours, preferably overnight.

4. Serve with pretzel sticks.

Poet Leslie Ullman, a fellow graduate of the University of Iowa, explained that her midwestern mother's highly pragmatic recipe turns out like a Jackson Pollack painting: "Rather colorful with the water chestnut and vegetable soup bits; especially delicious when you are starving at 2 a.m."

"Down Under" Crusty Cheese Cubes

MAKES: 8 servings

PREP. TIME: 10 minutes

BAKING TIME: 10 minutes

STANDING TIME: 6 hours, optional

Elizabeth Godfrey and I bonded on our first meeting at the Quaker retreat center beside the Cadbury chocolate factory in Bourneville, England. We shared food tales, mostly hers, growing out of her long-running cooking show on Australia TV. This recipe comes from The Best of Carefree Cooking, *her paperback of 100 recipes collected from 450 programs. She inscribed on the cover:* "For Willard Roth, with happy memories of cooking at Woodbrooke, March 1982."

INGREDIENTS:

2 or 3 slices stale bread

2 eggs

5 Tbsp. melted butter

¼ tsp. garlic salt

1 cup grated cheese of choice

1. Cut bread in 1″ squares.

2. In bowl, beat eggs with butter and garlic salt.

3. One at a time, dip bread cubes in egg mixture, roll in grated cheese, and set on ungreased baking sheet 1″ apart.

4. Bake at 400° until golden, about 10 minutes. Serve hot.

Tip: Cubes can be prepared ready for baking and refrigerated up to 6 hours ahead.

Orange Cream Dip with Fresh Fruit

MAKES: 24 servings (about 2 ½ cups)

PREP. TIME: 10 minutes

CHILLING TIME: 2 hours

INGREDIENTS:

1 ¼ cups milk

3-oz. package instant vanilla pudding mix

6-oz. can frozen orange juice, thawed

6 oz. vanilla Greek yogurt

3 Tbsp. triple sec liqueur, *optional*

assorted fresh colorful finger fruits of choice

fresh mint leaves

1. Place milk in bowl and add pudding mix until dissolved, then add undiluted orange juice. Mix with electric beater about 2 minutes.

2. Stir in yogurt and liqueur. Cover and chill at least 2 hours.

3. Arrange dip in center of platter and surround with fruit. Garnish with mint leaves.

Louisiana Sweet Potato Cheese Ball

MAKES: 24 servings (about 3 cups)

PREP. TIME: 45 minutes

CHILLING TIME: 8 hours

This recipe comes from the wife of a Louisiana sweet potato farmer, who used it at fairs and festivals to market family produce. It is labor intensive but guests will thank you for investing the effort.

INGREDIENTS:

8 oz. cream cheese, softened

2 cups sweet potatoes, cooked, mashed, and cooled

¼ cup finely chopped onion

3-oz. can green chilies, drained

1 tsp. seasoned salt

1 tsp. Worcestershire sauce

1 tsp. hot pepper sauce

¼ cup chopped pecans

crackers, breadsticks, or fresh vegetable sticks

1. In mixing bowl, beat cream cheese and sweet potatoes until smooth. Add remaining ingredients and mix well.
2. Cover and refrigerate 4 hours, or until easy to handle.
3. Shape into a ball, cover and refrigerate for 4 hours, or until firm.
4. Serve with crackers, breadsticks or vegetable sticks.

SOUPS

Bison Chili

For a slow cooker (ideal size: 7 qt.)

MAKES: 12 servings

PREP. TIME: 20 minutes

COOKING TIME: 3 to 5 hours

My own recipe using Midwestern bison and unsweetened chocolate.

INGREDIENTS:

1 ½ lb. ground bison

1 Tbsp. olive oil

1 tsp. ground cumin

1 Tbsp. chili powder

1 tsp. powdered garlic

1 ½ cups chopped onion

1 cup port, *divided*

4 15-oz. cans red kidney beans, *divided*

3 15-oz. cans diced tomatoes

⅓ cup dark brown sugar

4 1-oz. squares unsweetened baking chocolate (100% cacao)

1. In skillet, brown bison in oil with cumin, chili powder, garlic, onion, and ½ cup port for 15 minutes.

2. Spray slow cooker with canola or olive oil; turn on high. Put in 3 cans of beans with juice, and add meat mixture.

3. Using same skillet, warm tomatoes with brown sugar for 5 minutes. Add to slow cooker.

4. In same skillet, melt baking chocolate and combine with the additional can of beans. Add to slow cooker.

5. Deglaze skillet with ½ cup port and add to slow cooker.

6. Cook on high for 3 hours or low for 5. Serve hot.

Apricot Beef Sweet-Sour Soup

A Middle Eastern dish easily upgraded to a main course by serving in bowls with pita and a salad of choice.

MAKES: 10 1-cup servings or 4 bowls

PREP. TIME: 2 hours

COOKING TIME: 50 minutes

INGREDIENTS:

½ lb. lean ground beef sirloin

¼ cup minced onion

⅛ tsp. black pepper

⅛ tsp. ground cinnamon

¼ tsp. salt

2 quarts water

2 bouillon cubes, cook's choice

½ cup uncooked long-grain rice

1 cup dried apricots, cut in thin strips

1 cup pitted prunes, cut in half

15-oz. can garbanzo beans, drained and rinsed

¾ cup chopped fresh parsley

1 tsp. crumbled dried mint leaves

2 Tbsp. fresh lemon juice

1. In medium bowl, mix beef, onion, black pepper, cinnamon, and salt. Using a half-teaspoon measure, form into miniature meatballs.

2. Heat water with bouillon in 5-quart pan over high heat. Stir to dissolve bouillon. When boiling rapidly, add beef balls, rice, apricots, prunes, garbanzo beans, and parsley. Cover; reduce heat and simmer 40 minutes.

3. Remove from heat and stir in mint and lemon juice. Add more mint, lemon juice, and cinnamon to taste before serving.

Hawkeye Corn and Chilies Chowder

MAKES: 6 servings

PREP. TIME: 20 minutes, plus time to prepare Poblano chilies

COOKING TIME: 20 minutes

Roasted Poblano chilies add extra warmth to this dish using fresh sweet corn.

INGREDIENTS:

4 Poblano chilies

6 ears fresh sweet corn, or 4 cups frozen corn kernels

1 cup chopped onion

1 cup chopped celery

1 cup diced carrot

1 red bell pepper, chopped

2 cloves garlic, minced

2 Tbsp. olive oil

3 Tbsp. flour

2 14-oz. cans chicken broth

2 cups Yukon Gold potatoes, unpeeled, diced

1 Tbsp. freshly ground black pepper

1 tsp. salt

½ tsp. ground cumin

1 cup half-and-half *or* whole milk

butter

parsley

1. Roast Poblano chilies, remove skins and seeds, and chop.

2. Cut kernels from cob and scrape to remove pulp for enhanced flavor. Set aside.

3. In large heavy pan, sauté chilies, onion, celery, carrot, bell pepper, and garlic in olive oil over medium heat about 5 minutes.

4. Stir in flour and cook about 1 minute. Slowly stir in broth before adding corn, potatoes, black pepper, salt, and cumin. Bring to boil, stirring occasionally. Reduce heat to medium-low and cook until potatoes are tender, about 10 minutes. Stir in half-and-half.

5. Before serving, top individual bowls with a pat of sweet butter and fresh parsley.

Cool Cantaloupe Soup

Utterly simple, this soup comes from Chef Tim Carrigan at Fernwood Gardens Café, Niles, Michigan.

MAKES: 4 servings

PREP. TIME: 10 minutes

CHILLING TIME: 60 minutes

INGREDIENTS:

1 small cantaloupe, peeled and cubed

1 Tbsp. chopped fresh mint

1 Tbsp. honey

1 cup sparkling white grape juice

1. Puree ingredients in food processor or blender.

2. Refrigerate at least an hour before serving. Garnish with fresh strawberry slices.

Chilled Apple and Tomato Soup

MAKES: 8 servings

PREP. TIME: 15 minutes

CHILLING TIME: at least 15 minutes

A soothing summer soup adapted from the Park Hotel in County Kerry, Ireland.

INGREDIENTS:

12 ripe plum tomatoes, quartered, then halved

6 Granny Smith apples, cored and quartered

2 ¼ cups tomato juice

2 ¼ cups apple juice

12 fresh basil leaves, plus 8 leaves for garnish

1. Put all ingredients except basil leaves for garnish in blender, and blend until smooth.

2. Refrigerate until serving. Garnish each cup with basil leaf.

Chilled Melon Mint Soup

MAKES: 8 servings

PREP. TIME: 15 minutes

CHILLING TIME: 15 minutes

INGREDIENTS:

2 cups ripe honey dew, cut in 1" pieces

2 cups watermelon, cut in 1" pieces

6 oz. mint-berry Greek yogurt

¼ cup chopped fresh mint leaves

½ tsp. ground cumin

½ tsp. salt

1 Tbsp. fresh lime juice

3 Tbsp. triple sec or peach liqueur

¼ cup sesame seeds, toasted

4 mint sprigs

1. Blend all ingredients except sesame seeds in blender for 30–45 seconds.

2. Refrigerate 15 minutes. Stir and divide between four bowls.

3. Top with sesame seeds and a mint sprig before serving.

Tip: May be prepared 4–6 hours ahead.

Thai Coconut Shrimp Soup

MAKES: 4 servings (about 5 cups)

PREP. TIME: 10 minutes

COOKING TIME: 20 minutes

Unlike many Thai dishes, this is only mildly spicy. It is low in calories and easy to prepare.

INGREDIENTS:

3 cups low-sodium chicken broth

14-oz. can unsweetened light coconut milk

1 tsp. red curry paste

1 Tbsp. fish sauce

2 tsp. grated fresh ginger

1 garlic clove, crushed

½ tsp. sea salt

1 cup green beans (fresh *or* frozen), cut in 1" pieces

12 oz. medium shrimp (fresh or frozen), peeled and deveined

2 green onions, thinly sliced

1. In pot over medium-high heat, combine chicken broth, coconut milk, red curry paste, fish sauce, ginger, garlic, and salt. Bring to boil, then reduce heat to medium-low.

2. Add beans and cook 2 minutes. Add shrimp and cook 5 minutes more.

3. Divide between four bowls, garnish with green onions, and serve.

Oyster Stew

MAKES: 6 servings

PREP. TIME: 10 minutes

COOKING TIME: 10 minutes

INGREDIENTS:

¼ cup butter

16 oz. fresh standard oysters

½ tsp. salt

¼ tsp. freshly ground black pepper

2 quarts milk

1. In pan over medium heat, melt butter and add oysters in their liquid, salt, and pepper.

2. When the edges of the oysters curl, add milk and heat to boiling, stirring occasionally to keep from scorching.

Tip: To enhance flavor, make stew ahead and keep on low heat (not simmering). Turn heat up just before serving.

Once a year Grandfather Ben Roth ordered a gallon of fresh oysters at the Wayland (Iowa) Grocery for family Christmas festivities. Christmas Eve supper was simple: oyster stew with saltines, Longhorn cheese and home-canned sweet pickles with a holiday dessert. My father Elmer saw to it that his children had the same opportunity.

Red Potato and Carrot Chowder

MAKES: 8 servings

PREP. TIME: 15 minutes

COOKING TIME: 30 minutes

INGREDIENTS:

3 cups diced, unpeeled red potatoes (about 5 medium)

1 cup grated carrot

½ cup chopped celery

½ cup chopped red onion

2 cups vegetable broth

1 cup water, boiling

3 Tbsp. butter

⅓ cup flour

1 ½ cups milk

1 cup shredded cheese of choice

4 green onions, sliced

1. Combine vegetables, broth, and water in pot over medium heat. Bring to boil, cover, and simmer 10 minutes.

2. In small skillet, melt butter over medium heat, stir in flour and add milk slowly, cooking until thick. Add cheese and stir well until melted.

3. Add cheese sauce to cooked vegetables and cook 5 minutes on medium-high.

4. Ladle into serving bowls. Top with green onions.

SALADS

Panzanella

MAKES: 6–8 servings

PREP. TIME: 15 minutes

RESTING TIME: 30 minutes to 4 hours

Tradition has it that this Tuscan salad was designed to use up old, crusty bread while showcasing luscious tomatoes. This recipe is simply a base for departure; amounts can vary according to availability and your taste.

INGREDIENTS:

4 cups tomatoes, cut into large chunks, some seeds removed

4 cups day-old crusty bread, chunks same size as tomato chunks

1 cucumber, peeled and seeded, cut into large chunks

½ red onion, chopped

1 bunch fresh basil, torn into small pieces

¼ cup olive oil

Salt and pepper to taste

½ cup pitted black olives, *optional*

1. In large bowl with cover, combine all ingredients. Marinate covered, without refrigeration, at least 30 minutes and up to 4 hours.

2. Serve at room temperature.

Columbia Gorge Spinach Salad

MAKES: 10–12 servings

PREP. TIME: 15 minutes

CHILLING TIME: 8 hours or overnight

Inspired by an old recipe from the Columbia River Gorge Hotel, a historic Oregon landmark continuing to provide hospitality.

INGREDIENTS:

12 oz. fresh baby spinach

4 slices turkey bacon, crushed

4 oz. bean sprouts

2 ribs celery, chopped

5 green onions, sliced

12 oz. garden peas, frozen

4 oz. cheddar cheese, shredded

⅓ cup sour cream

⅓ cup light mayonnaise

⅓ cup low-fat yogurt

⅓ cup confectioners sugar

8-oz. can sliced water chestnuts, drained

1. Layer spinach, bacon, bean sprouts, celery, green onions, peas, and shredded cheese, in order, into a 9" x 13" baking dish.

2. "Frost" with a dressing of sour cream, mayonnaise, yogurt and confectioners sugar.

3. Top with water chestnuts.

4. Refrigerate at least 8 hours, or overnight, before serving.

English Cucumber and Onions

MAKES: 6 servings

PREP. TIME: 10 minutes

CHILLING TIME: 2 hours

This recipe was given to us by a friend we have known since we lived in Ghana decades ago. We added the second-day adaptation, a pasta salad.

INGREDIENTS:

¼ cup seasoned rice vinegar

¼ cup sugar

1 English cucumber, thinly sliced

1 medium red onion, thinly sliced

⅛ tsp. red pepper flakes

¼ tsp. salt

⅛ tsp. black pepper

Grated peel of 1 lime

1. Mix vinegar and sugar until sugar is dissolved. Combine with remaining ingredients.
2. Refrigerate 2 hours before serving.

Tip: This second-day adaptation uses half of the original recipe: Drain vinegar dressing from leftover salad, reserving ¼ cup of the liquid. Add 1 Tbsp. olive oil to the cucumbers, and toss with 8 oz. of your favorite pasta, cooked and cooled. Fresh chopped basil is optional. Chill 30 minutes and add reserved dressing just before serving. Serves 3–4.

Spinach Pear Salad with Warm Vinaigrette

MAKES: 6 servings

PREP. TIME: 10 minutes

INGREDIENTS:

10 oz. fresh baby spinach

3 Tbsp. crumbled blue or feta cheese

¼ red onion, thinly sliced

16-oz. can pear slices, drained; reserve juice for dressing

3 Tbsp. juice from pears

3 Tbsp. white balsamic vinegar

3 Tbsp. olive oil

¼ tsp. salt

¼ tsp. pepper

1. Wash and dry spinach. Put in salad bowl, sprinkle with cheese and onion; top with pear slices.

2. In small saucepan, heat juice, vinegar, and oil until mixture is steaming. Pour dressing immediately over salad.

3. Toss tableside until evenly dressed; season with freshly ground salt and pepper. Serve at once.

Tip: Use microwave for making dressing.

Carrot, Raisin, and Yogurt Slaw

MAKES: 3 servings

PREP. TIME: 15 minutes

INGREDIENTS:

4 carrots, shredded

1 small bunch cilantro, chopped

1 cup low-fat Greek yogurt

¼ cup golden raisins

1 garlic clove, minced

1 tsp. lemon juice

Dash of Worcestershire sauce

Salt and freshly ground pepper, *optional*

1. Combine all ingredients in a bowl and mix well.
2. Divide equally between three individual dishes.

Broccoli Couscous Salad

MAKES: 6–8 servings

PREP. TIME: 15 minutes

CHILLING TIME: 30 minutes

INGREDIENTS:

1 cup dry couscous

½ tsp. sea salt

¼ tsp. black pepper + to taste for dressing

1 bay leaf

2 cups fresh orange juice

2 tsp. coarse country-style mustard

1 Tbsp. olive oil

3 cups steamed broccoli, in 1-inch pieces, chilled

1 Tbsp. chopped fresh chives

1 Tbsp. chopped fresh mint

1 cup chopped, toasted almonds

Lettuce leaves

1. Prepare couscous according to package directions (usually, bring 1 ¼ cups water to boil, add 1 cup couscous, remove from heat and let stand covered for 5 minutes; fluff with fork). Add salt, pepper, and bay leaf to boiling water with couscous. Let this cool about 30 minutes.

2. While couscous cools, prepare dressing: Simmer orange juice in small saucepan over low heat until reduced to ½ cup. Stir in mustard, olive oil, and black pepper to taste. Cool about 30 minutes.

3. In large bowl, combine cooled couscous, chilled broccoli, chives, and mint. Toss gently with half the orange dressing.

4. Serve over lettuce, drizzle with remaining dressing, and top with almonds. Garnish with additional mint if desired.

Endive with Goat Cheese and Walnuts

MAKES: 8 servings

PREP. TIME: 10 minutes

INGREDIENTS:

2 heads endive

8 oz. soft goat cheese

3 Tbsp. walnuts, chopped

Honey to drizzle

1. Wash and dry endive, and separate leaves. Arrange large outer leaves on a serving platter.

2. Spoon a teaspoon of goat cheese on each leaf, then sprinkle with walnuts and drizzle with honey.

Beet Slaw

MAKES: 6 servings

PREP. TIME: 15 minutes

CHILLING TIME: optional

INGREDIENTS:

½ Tbsp. sherry vinegar

1 ½ Tbsp. fine-cut orange marmalade

2 15-oz. cans whole beets, drained and shredded

1 scallion, thinly sliced

¼ cup golden raisins

¼ tsp. salt

¼ tsp. ground black pepper

1. In a large bowl, stir vinegar and marmalade to combine.

2. Add other ingredients and mix gently.

3. Serve immediately or refrigerate.

Red Beets and Eggs

MAKES: 8–10 servings

PREP. TIME: 45 minutes

CHILLING TIME: 4–8 hours

This is noted as "an old family recipe" by a contributor to my Aunt Lucille's Coffee Cup Cookbook.

INGREDIENTS:

6–8 tender young beets

1 cup water

½ cup vinegar

¼ cup brown sugar

½ cinnamon stick

3 whole cloves

6 hard-cooked eggs, shells removed

1. Wash beets, remove tops but leave about 2″ of stems. Cover with water and cook about 30 minutes, or until easily pierced with a fork. Cool and peel.

2. Meanwhile, bring to a boil the water, vinegar, sugar, cinnamon, and cloves. Stir until sugar is dissolved.

3. Place beets and eggs in a bowl, and cover with the hot liquid. Cool and chill 4–8 hours, turning eggs and beets several times so they marinate evenly.

4. To serve, drain beets and eggs; cut eggs in half and arrange on platter with sliced beets.

SMALL PLATES

Corn Leek Bake

MAKES: 8 servings

PREP. TIME: 15 minutes

BAKING TIME: 35 minutes

STANDING TIME: 5 minutes

INGREDIENTS:

2 leeks, white and pale green parts

2 Tbsp. butter

4 eggs

3 Tbsp. cornstarch

2 Tbsp. sugar

1 tsp. nutmeg *or* mace

¼ tsp. red pepper

½ cup whole milk

16-oz. can creamed corn

16-oz. can whole kernel corn, drained

1 cup cheese of cook's choice, shredded

1. Cut leeks lengthwise, slice crosswise, rinse well and drain; you should have about 1 cup. In saucepan, sauté leeks in butter over medium heat about 3 minutes; remove from stove.

2. In bowl, whisk eggs. Blend cornstarch, sugar, and spices into milk (I prefer shaking in a covered jar) and whisk into eggs. Stir in leeks and corn.

3. Pour into greased 8″ x 11″ baking pan. Top with cheese.

4. Bake at 350° for 35 minutes. Remove from oven and let stand at least 5 minutes before serving.

Cabbage Au Gratin

MAKES: 6–8 servings

PREP. TIME: 10 minutes

BAKING TIME: 30 minutes

This is a southern culinary staple at Berea College's Boone Tavern Hotel in Kentucky, where students work in the kitchen and dining room as part of earning and learning.

INGREDIENTS:

1 quart shredded cabbage

¾ cup water

½ tsp. salt

7 Tbsp. butter, *divided*

¼ cup all-purpose flour

2 ¼ cups milk, hot

½ tsp. salt

½ tsp. pepper

⅔ cup grated cheddar cheese, *divided*

1 slice day-old bread, cut into tiny cubes to make crumbs

1. In saucepan, place cabbage in boiling salted water. Cook until cabbage has wilted (about 5 minutes).

2. Meanwhile make white sauce: Melt 4 Tbsp. (half stick) butter in small saucepan. Add flour and cook for 3 minutes, stirring constantly. Add hot milk slowly, continuing to cook and stir until sauce is thickened and smooth (about 5 minutes). Add salt and pepper. This will make about 2 ½ cups sauce.

3. When sauce is cooked, stir in ⅓ cup cheese and add wilted cabbage. Mix and place in well-greased 2-quart casserole. Distribute remainder of cheese over top.

4. In small skillet, brown bread crumbs in 3 Tbsp. melted butter; sprinkle over cheese.

5. Bake at 400° for 30 minutes.

Whole Wheat Couscous with Goat Cheese and Plums

Accented by fresh mint and sliced scallions, this plate is simple yet superb.

MAKES: 6 servings

PREP. TIME: 10 minutes

RESTING TIME: 10 minutes

COOKING TIME: 10 minutes

INGREDIENTS:

1 ½ cups water

1 cup couscous (whole wheat preferred)

3 ripe plums, pitted and chopped

2 scallions, thinly sliced

2 oz. goat cheese, crumbled (aged preferred)

½ cup chopped fresh mint

3 Tbsp. honey

3 ½ Tbsp. balsamic vinegar

salt

pepper

1. Bring water to a boil in medium saucepan. Add couscous, stir, and turn off heat. Cover and let rest for 10 minutes.

2. Fluff couscous with a fork. Transfer to a medium bowl. When cool, add plums, scallions, cheese, and mint.

3. Whisk honey and vinegar in a small bowl until honey is dissolved. Pour mixture over couscous, and toss gently. Season with salt and pepper to taste.

Roasted Tomatoes with Herbed Ricotta and Walnuts

MAKES: 4 servings

PREP. AND BAKING TIME: 2 ½ hours start to finish, 30 minutes active

INGREDIENTS:

- 4 large tomatoes, halved and cored
- ¼ tsp. salt
- ½ tsp. sugar
- ¼ tsp. ground white pepper
- 1 cup low-fat ricotta cheese
- 1 Tbsp. chopped fresh basil
- 2 tsp. chopped fresh thyme
- 2 tsp. chopped fresh oregano
- ¼ cup chopped walnuts, toasted
- 2 Tbsp. balsamic vinegar

1. Heat oven to 325°. Place a wire rack over a rimmed baking sheet. Spray the rack with cooking spray.

2. Arrange tomatoes on the rack, cut sides up. Sprinkle with the salt, sugar, and white pepper. Roast for 1 hour. Flip tomatoes over and roast for another hour, or until the tomatoes are soft, wrinkly, and have shrunken considerably in size.

3. While the tomatoes are roasting, in a medium bowl stir together the ricotta and the three herbs. Set aside to allow flavors to meld.

4. Serve the herbed ricotta alongside the roasted tomato halves. Sprinkle with toasted walnuts and drizzle lightly with balsamic vinegar.

Jhinga Biryani

MAKES: 10 servings

PREP. TIME: 30 minutes

CHILLING TIME: 1 hour

RESTING TIME: 1 hour

BAKING TIME: 45–60 minutes

This baked spicy rice with coconut and shrimp offers an oriental accent.

INGREDIENTS:

1 lb. shrimp, with tails

2 tsp. coarse salt, *divided*

½ tsp. ground red pepper

¼ tsp. turmeric

1 cup basmati rice

2 Tbsp. olive oil

1 tsp. cumin

1 tsp. fennel seeds

12 oz. fresh greens (spinach, kale, endive or combination)

½ cup shredded coconut, covered with ½ cup boiling water for 15 minutes, then drained

4 Tbsp. unsalted butter (half stick), *divided*

½ cup raw cashews

½ cup golden raisins

2 cardamom pods

2 cinnamon sticks

2 bay leaves

1 red onion, cut in half and thinly sliced

½ tsp. saffron threads

1 ½ cups water

1. Combine shrimp, 1 tsp. salt, red pepper, and turmeric; refrigerate, covered, at least 1 hour.

2. Soak rice in enough water to cover, set aside at room temperature for 1 hour, and drain.

3. Heat oil in large skillet over medium heat. Sprinkle in cumin and fennel seeds until they sizzle, turn reddish brown, and smell nutty and sweet (10–15 seconds). Add greens by handfuls, stirring until wilted. Stir in shrimp and coconut, and remove from heat.

4. Heat 2 Tbsp. butter in medium skillet over medium heat. Add cashews and raisins, stirring 3 minutes; using slotted spoon, transfer nuts and raisins to a plate.

5. Put remaining butter in same skillet, adding cardamom, cinnamon, bay leaves, and onion. Cook, stirring, 3–5 minutes. Add drained rice and saffron. Stir-fry to coat. Add water and remaining salt. Bring to boil, cook until craters appear in rice (5–8 minutes). Remove from heat.

6. Spray 2-quart casserole with non-stick cooking spray. Spoon half shrimp mixture to form bottom layer. Add half the rice to form second layer. Repeat layers.

7. Cover and bake at 350° for 45–60 minutes. Remove from oven, and sprinkle cashews and raisins over top. When serving, scoop from all 4 layers.

Tip: Remind guests not to eat whole spices.

Escalloped Corn with Oysters

MAKES: 12 servings

PREP. TIME: 10 minutes

BAKING TIME: 45–50 minutes

A holiday family favorite for the oyster lovers in seacoast-deprived Iowa.

INGREDIENTS:

2 eggs, beaten

2 cups milk

16-oz. can whole kernel corn, drained

16-oz. can creamed corn

4 oz. saltines (1 sleeve), crushed

1 tsp. black pepper

16-oz can fresh oysters

1. In greased 2-quart casserole, mix all ingredients thoroughly, in order given.
2. Bake at 350° for 45–50 minutes.

Curried Rice with Apples and Peas

MAKES: 4 servings

PREP. TIME: 15 minutes

COOKING TIME: 25 minutes

INGREDIENTS:

2 Tbsp. butter, *divided*

1 cup quick-cooking rice

½ cup finely chopped onion

1 tsp. finely chopped garlic

1 medium apple, peeled and cored, finely chopped

2 tsp. curry powder

½ tsp. salt

1 ½ cups water

1 bay leaf

¾ cup frozen peas, thawed under hot water

1. Melt 1 Tbsp. butter in saucepan. Add rice, onion, garlic, apple, curry powder, and salt. Cook briefly, stirring, but do not brown.

2. Add water and bay leaf. Bring to boil, stirring. Cover tightly, lower heat and simmer 15 minutes.

3. Remove from heat. Add the peas and remaining 1 Tbsp. butter. Fluff rice with a fork, discard bay leaf, and serve.

Cheese Grits with Chunky Tomato Sauce

MAKES: 6 servings

PREP. TIME: 10 minutes

COOKING TIME: 30 minutes

Thanks to our native American siblings, we can savor hominy turned to grits.

INGREDIENTS:

2 tsp. olive oil

1 small onion, chopped

15-oz. can diced Italian-style tomatoes

¼ tsp. red pepper flakes

½ tsp. garlic powder

4 cups low-fat milk

1 cup yellow old-fashioned *or* quick grits

1 cup shredded reduced-fat Cheddar cheese

¼ tsp. ground black pepper

1. Heat oil in saucepan over medium heat. Add onion and sauté 6 minutes. Reduce heat to medium-low, and stir in tomatoes, pepper flakes, and garlic powder. Simmer 12 minutes.

2. Mash sauce with potato masher until chunky-smooth. Remove from heat, and cover to keep warm.

3. Whisk together milk and grits in large saucepan over medium-low heat. Cook 6–8 minutes, until soft and thick. Stir in cheese and pepper.

4. Spoon grits into shallow serving bowls. Top with warm tomato sauce.

Chilled Marinated Asparagus

Mary Finke provided this starter for the 2004 recipe collection by Columbus Mennonite Church in Ohio.

MAKES: 6–8 servings

PREP. TIME: 5 minutes

COOKING TIME: 9 minutes

CHILLING TIME: 2 hours

INGREDIENTS:

2 lbs. fresh asparagus

1 tsp. salt

MARINADE:

½ cup olive oil

3 Tbsp. white wine vinegar

3 Tbsp. chopped fresh parsley + additional for garnish

2-oz. jar pimentos, chopped

2 Tbsp. chopped fresh chives, *or* scallions

½ tsp. salt

¼ tsp. freshly ground pepper

tomato rose, *optional*

1. Remove tough ends of asparagus, and remove scales from stalks with knife or peeler.

2. Cover asparagus with boiling water. Add salt and simmer 6–9 minutes until crisp-tender. Drain. Rinse with cold water and drain again. Place in shallow container.

3. Whisk together oil, vinegar, 3 Tbsp. parsley, pimentos, chives, salt, and pepper. Pour this marinade over asparagus. Cover and chill at least 2 hours.

4. To serve, arrange asparagus spears in circular pattern on large round platter. Drizzle marinade in wide ribbon over asparagus. Garnish with parsley, and tomato rose if desired.

Eight decades as host and guest at home and away
1943–1952

Angel food cakes with cooked burnt sugar frosting followed me to college. Mother found a willing driver to deliver the traditional cake to her eldest in his first year at Hesston College in Kansas. When the unexpected specialty came I invited several close friends to join my seven housemates to share. When a new friend from Oregon asked what the cake variety was, I was confused. "I just told you, it's my birthday cake." "I know," my friend replied, "but is it white, yellow, or brown?" I was flabbergasted. For the first time in nineteen years, I became aware that birthday cakes came, like Joseph's coat, in many colors.

MAINS

CHEESE, EGG, AND PASTA

Spinach and Ricotta Penne

MAKES: 4 servings

PREP. TIME: 10 minutes

COOKING TIME: 10 minutes

Combine baby spinach, ricotta cheese and pasta for a savory dish.

INGREDIENTS:

8 oz. pasta, penne or ziti

12 oz. fresh baby spinach

1 cup whole-milk ricotta cheese

¼ tsp. salt

¼ tsp. freshly ground black pepper

1. In large saucepan, bring lightly salted water to a boil and cook pasta until al dente.

2. Reserving 2 cups of the pasta cooking water, drain pasta and transfer to large serving bowl.

3. Add just enough pasta water to ricotta to create a smooth sauce, and stir in spinach.

4. Toss until spinach wilts, adding salt and pepper. Serve immediately.

Corn Macaroni Deluxe

MAKES: 8 servings

PREP. TIME: 10 minutes

COOKING TIME: 30 minutes or 4 hours

Choose microwave, oven, or slow cooker to cook together corn, pasta, and cheese for "mac and cheese" with a difference.

INGREDIENTS:

16-oz. can whole kernel corn

16-oz. can creamed corn

1 ¼ cup whole wheat pasta, dry (macaroni *or* rotini)

½ cup butter (1 stick)

1 cup shredded sharp cheddar cheese

1. Combine all ingredients; spoon into greased 9″ x 13″ pan for oven or microwave, or greased slow cooker.

2. Cooking times:
   - Conventional oven—bake at 350° for 30 minutes.
   - Microwave—30 minutes on high, stirring every 5 minutes.
   - Slow cooker—4 hours on low, stirring midway.

Pasta with Walnuts and Parsley

MAKES: 4 servings

PREP. AND COOKING TIME: 45 minutes

INGREDIENTS:

1 cup chopped walnuts

16 oz. whole-wheat pasta

¼ cup olive oil

4 cloves garlic, minced

⅔ cup chopped fresh flat-leaf parsley + extra for garnish

¼ tsp. salt

½ tsp. freshly ground black pepper

1 cup freshly grated Parmesan cheese, *divided*

1. Have measured ingredients near the stove. Bring a large pot of salted water to boil.

2. In a large skillet over medium-high heat, toast walnuts until fragrant, 3–5 minutes, stirring frequently. Remove from skillet and set aside.

3. Add pasta to large pan of boiling water. While it cooks, add olive oil and garlic to skillet; stir over low heat 3–4 minutes, until garlic is soft and fragrant, being careful not to burn.

4. When pasta is almost al dente, drain, reserving ½ cup of the water.

5. Add drained pasta to skillet with reserved water, walnuts (reserving 3 Tbsp.), parsley, salt, and pepper. Toss to combine, cooking over low heat for 2 more minutes.

6. Turn off heat. Add ¾ cup of Parmesan cheese and toss to combine.

7. Pour into serving bowl or divide among 4 individual bowls. Top with remaining cheese and walnuts. Garnish with parsley.

Brown Rice with Pecans and Apples

MAKES: 8 servings

PREP. TIME: 10 minutes

BAKING TIME: 30 minutes

STANDING TIME: 5 minutes

INGREDIENTS:

1 tsp. oil

1 cup chopped onion

1 cup sliced fresh
   mushrooms

3 cups brown rice, cooked

¼ cup chicken broth
   (fat-free if desired)

1 small red apple, cored
   and chopped

3 Tbsp. chopped pecans

1 tsp. poultry seasoning

1. Heat oil in large nonstick skillet on medium-high. Add onions and mushrooms and cook 3 minutes, or until onion is golden.

2. In a 3-quart baking dish, combine onion mixture and remaining ingredients, mixing well.

3. Cover and bake 30 minutes at 350°. Remove from oven, cool 5 minutes, fluff with fork and serve.

Lemon Turkey Stir-Fry with Pasta

MAKES: 6 servings

PREP. TIME: 15 minutes

CHILLING TIME: 30 minutes

COOKING TIME: 10 minutes

INGREDIENTS:

1 ½ lb. turkey cutlets or slices, cut in ½" strips

1 Tbsp. soy sauce

1 Tbsp. white wine vinegar

2 tsp. cornstarch

1 tsp. lemon pepper

2 Tbsp. olive oil

6 green onions, sliced

1 fresh lemon, cut into 10 thin slices and finely slivered + extra slices for garnish

1 garlic clove, finely minced

10 oz. fresh spinach, cleaned and chopped

1 lb. linguine, prepared to package directions and drained

Parsley

1. In plastic bag, combine first turkey, soy sauce, vinegar, cornstarch, and pepper. Close bag and shake to coat turkey. Refrigerate 30 minutes to blend flavors.

2. In large non-stick skillet over medium heat, sauté turkey and marinade in oil for 2–3 minutes, or until meat is no longer pink in center. Add onions, lemon slivers, and garlic, continuing to cook until onions are translucent. Stir in spinach and cook until just wilted.

3. To serve, combine turkey mixture with hot linguine and garnish with parsley and lemon slices.

Quinoa and Corn Griddle Cakes with Black Bean Salsa

MAKES: 8 servings

PREP. TIME: 20 minutes

STANDING TIME: 1 hour

COOKING TIME: 30 minutes

INGREDIENTS:

BLACK BEAN SALSA:

15-oz. can black beans, rinsed and drained

1 ½ cups grape or cherry tomatoes, halved

1 jalapeno pepper, finely chopped

¼ cup finely chopped fresh cilantro or parsley

¼ cup finely chopped onion

¼ cup finely chopped red bell pepper

2 Tbsp. white wine vinegar

1 tsp. olive oil

⅛ tsp. salt

⅛ tsp. freshly ground black pepper

GRIDDLE CAKES:

½ cup quinoa, rinsed and drained

½ cup water

½ cup chicken or vegetable broth

1 egg, beaten

½ cup frozen corn kernels, thawed

2 scallions, finely chopped (¼ cup)

¼ cup shredded mozzarella cheese

¼ cup whole wheat flour

1 Tbsp. milk or buttermilk

¼ tsp. salt

⅛ tsp. hot pepper sauce

⅛ tsp. freshly ground black pepper

2 Tbsp. canola oil

Mix all ingredients and set aside at least 1 hour before serving with griddle cakes.

1. Mix quinoa, water, and broth in small saucepan; bring to a boil. Cover, reduce heat and simmer 15 minutes. Fluff with fork.

2. Combine quinoa and remaining ingredients, except oil, in medium bowl.

3. Heat oil in large skillet over medium-high heat. Scoop a generous ¼ cup of mixture at a time, and drop into skillet or on to griddle, flattening into pancake shape. Cook until browned on bottom, about 3 minutes, then flip carefully and cook about 3 minutes longer. Serve with salsa.

Spanish Potato Omelet (*Tortilla Española*)

MAKES: 6 servings

PREP. TIME: 10 minutes

STANDING TIME: 20 minutes

COOKING TIME: 15 minutes

INGREDIENTS:

6 eggs

5 medium potatoes, washed and sliced thinly

¼ tsp. salt

½ tsp. freshly ground black pepper

4 Tbsp. olive oil, divided

2 Tbsp. finely chopped onion

1. In bowl, beat eggs; add potatoes and seasonings. Let stand for 20 minutes.

2. Heat 2 Tbsp. oil in medium-size skillet on high heat. Add potatoes and cover. Check every few minutes to ensure they don't stick together and burn on edges. As potatoes soften, add onion. Cook for 3 more minutes. Remove from heat and blend.

3. In another medium-size skillet, heat 2 Tbsp. oil on high heat. When very hot, add potato and egg mixture and turn heat down to medium. When omelet begins to thicken, flip it onto a large plate, then slide back into skillet. Flip at least 2 more times until firm.

4. Cut in wedges and serve with a salad.

Plain Basic Omelet

MAKES: 1 serving

PREP. TIME: 5 minutes

COOKING TIME: 5 minutes

INGREDIENTS:

3 eggs

1 Tbsp. cold water or white wine

3 drops hot pepper sauce

⅛ tsp. salt

1 Tbsp. salted butter

1. Beat or whisk eggs with water or white wine, hot pepper sauce, and salt until eggs begin to foam; properly beaten, they make threads when lifted.

2. Heat skillet over medium heat. Flick a few drops of water onto skillet to test; when the drops jump around, the skillet is ready. Add butter. Pour eggs into hot pan.

3. With flat side of fork, make circular motions around bottom of pan fast. Speed is of the essence for a light and fluffy omelet. While the right hand makes a circular motion, shake the pan with the left hand, rocking back and forth, to keep eggs loose. When eggs are cooked and all liquid is firm, spread eggs evenly but lightly with a fork to cover any surface breaks. Pause briefly to let eggs set.

4. Turn omelet out by grasping the skillet handle with left hand, palm side up. Tilt skillet 45°, and with fork in right hand, roll omelet onto serving plate.

My teacher for omelet making was Rudy Stanish, "the omelet king" of southwestern Pennsylvania during a 2004 Cooking Time exposition at Westmoreland County Community College. Never add milk or cream to your eggs, he emphasized, only cold water or white wine. He proudly noted that Jackie engaged his skill for JFK's inaugural breakfast. Rudy's title came after he made omelets for Princess Diana. He died at 94 after a fall in his home near Pittsburgh in 2008.

Egyptian Lentils, Macaroni, and Rice (*Kushari*)

MAKES: 4–6 servings

PREP. TIME: 15 minutes

COOKING TIME: 45 minutes

INGREDIENTS:

1 cup long grain white rice

1 cup whole wheat macaroni

1 cup red lentils

3 Tbsp. oil, *divided*

2 large onions, chopped, *divided*

2 cloves garlic, minced

3 tomatoes, chopped

½ tsp. salt

½ tsp. cayenne pepper

¾ cup water

1 Tbsp. vinegar

1. Cook rice, macaroni, and lentils separately according to directions; drain.

2. In saucepan, sauté 1 onion in 1 Tbsp. oil; transfer to small bowl and set aside.

3. In same pan, sauté 1 onion and garlic in 2 Tbsp. oil. Add tomatoes, salt, and cayenne pepper and cook 3 minutes, then add water and simmer 5–10 minutes. Remove from heat and add vinegar.

4. In individual bowls layer (in order) rice, macaroni and lentils. Cover with tomato sauce and top with onions.

VEGETARIAN

Sweet Potato Lasagna

MAKES: 6–8 servings

PREP. TIME: 20 minutes

STEAMING TIME: 5 minutes

BAKING TIME: 1 hour

STANDING TIME: 10 minutes

Packed with protein, this recipe calls for sweet potatoes rather than lasagna noodles.

INGREDIENTS:

3 medium sweet potatoes

1 lb. fresh spinach

9 oz. firm tofu

1 cup low-fat ricotta cheese

1 ½ tsp. dried oregano

½ tsp. dried basil

¼ cup chopped fresh parsley

2 cloves garlic, minced

32-oz. jar tomato sauce

8 oz. shredded mozzarella cheese

3 Tbsp. wheat germ, *optional*

1. Peel and thinly slice sweet potatoes. Lightly steam spinach and drain. Set both aside.

2. Prepare filling: Drain tofu but do not squeeze out water. Blend tofu and ricotta in blender until smooth. Add oregano, basil, parsley, and garlic; blend enough to mix.

3. To assemble: Layer ⅓ of the tomato sauce then half the sliced potatoes, spinach, filling, mozzarella. Repeat this, but layer in the final ⅓ of the tomato sauce before the final mozzarella. Sprinkle wheat germ over top.

4. Bake at 375° for 1 hour. Remove and let stand 10 minutes before serving.

Monastery Cornbread Casserole

MAKES: 6 servings

PREP. TIME: 10 minutes

BAKING TIME: 30 minutes

STANDING TIME: 5 minutes

This staple originates from the monks at Mepkin Abbey in South Carolina, simplified for a lay kitchen.

INGREDIENTS:

1 cup yellow cornmeal

1 ½ tsp. baking powder

¼ tsp. salt

2 eggs, lightly beaten

¾ cup sour cream *or* yogurt

½ cup olive oil

12-oz. package frozen corn kernels, thawed

1 cup shredded sharp cheddar cheese

4-oz. can green chilies, medium hot

1 Tbsp. chili powder

1. In bowl, combine cornmeal, baking powder, and salt. Add eggs, sour cream, and oil, and blend well; stir in corn.
2. Heat a greased 10″ cast iron skillet in a 375° oven for 3 minutes. Pour half the batter into pre-heated skillet; cover with cheese and green chilies.
3. Spoon remaining batter on top, then sprinkle with chili powder.
4. Return skillet to oven and bake for 25 minutes, or until lightly browned.
5. Remove and cool 5 minutes. Cut in six wedges and serve with salad of choice.

Tip: A dash or two of hot pepper sauce added to the chilies enhances heat for the hearty.

Vegetarian Peanut Stew

For a slow cooker (ideal size: 5 qt.)

MAKES: 8 servings

PREP. TIME: 15 minutes

COOKING TIME: 4–5 hours on high

INGREDIENTS:

3 cloves garlic

2 cups loosely filled cilantro, leaves and stems

28-oz. can diced tomatoes

½ cup peanut butter (chunky preferable)

2 tsp. ground cumin

½ tsp. ground cinnamon

¼ tsp. cayenne pepper (or to taste)

¼ tsp. salt

1 cup water

4 medium sweet potatoes, cut in 2" chunks (about 3 lbs.)

15-oz. can garbanzo beans, drained

16-oz. package frozen green beans

1. Combine garlic, cilantro, tomatoes, peanut butter, cumin, cinnamon, cayenne pepper, and salt in blender or food processor. Blend to puree, then pour into slow cooker.

2. Add water, potatoes and garbanzo beans.

3. Cook 8–10 hours on low or 4–5 hours on high.

4. Cook green beans separately and add to stew 5 minutes before serving.

Hearty Polenta Florentine

MAKES: 4 servings

PREP. AND COOKING TIME: 10 minutes

INGREDIENTS:

1 tsp. olive oil

2 cloves garlic, minced

½ cup fat-free, low-sodium vegetable broth

¼ cup oil-packed sun-dried tomato halves, drained and chopped

½ tsp. ground cumin

15-oz. can black beans, rinsed and drained

16-oz. package fresh baby spinach

4 cups water

1 cup uncooked polenta

1 Tbsp. butter

½ tsp. salt

¾ cup (3 oz.) crumbled goat cheese

½ tsp. freshly ground black pepper

1. Heat oil in large skillet on medium-high heat. Sauté garlic 1 minute or until golden. Stir in broth, sun-dried tomatoes, cumin, and black beans. Bring to a simmer and cook 2 minutes, stirring occasionally. Remove from heat, add spinach and toss to combine.

2. Bring water to a boil in medium saucepan. Whisk into water the polenta, butter, and salt. Reduce heat; simmer 3 minutes or until thick, stirring constantly.

3. Spoon ¼ cup polenta into each of 4 bowls, top each with ¾ cup of bean mixture. Top each bowl with 3 Tbsp. of the cheese. Garnish with black pepper as desired.

Vegetarian Lasagna Florentine

MAKES: 10 servings

PREP. TIME:

BAKING TIME: 45 minutes

STANDING TIME: 5 minutes

Cousin Ruth's béchamel sauce combined with spinach in abundance—oh, so good.

INGREDIENTS:

12 oz. lasagna noodles

TOMATO SAUCE:

1 ½ cups sliced fresh mushrooms

1 onion, chopped

1 cup tomato sauce

¼ tsp. garlic powder

¼ tsp. salt

¼ tsp. freshly ground black pepper

CHEESE MIXTURE:

12 oz. ricotta cheese

1 egg

3 cups chopped fresh baby spinach

2 Tbsp. chopped fresh basil

2 Tbsp. chopped fresh chives

BÉCHAMEL SAUCE:

2 Tbsp. butter

2 Tbsp. flour

1 cup milk

¼ tsp. salt

¼ tsp. freshly ground black pepper

½ cup grated fresh Parmesan cheese

1. Cook lasagna noodles according to package directions. Drain and set aside.

2. Combine tomato sauce ingredients in saucepan, and simmer on medium heat for 10 minutes. Set aside.

3. Combine ingredients for cheese mixture and set aside.

4. Make béchamel sauce: in medium saucepan over medium heat melt butter; stir in flour until smooth, then continue cooking until sand-colored, from 5 to 7 minutes. In separate pan, heat milk then add to butter-flour mixture, whisking until smooth; continue cooking for 10 minutes, stirring constantly. Remove from heat and add seasonings.

5. Combine cheese mixture with ¾ cup béchamel sauce.

6. In a greased 9" x 13" pan, layer the lasagna in the following order:
   - Layer of cooked noodles on bottom
   - Cheese and béchamel mixture
   - Another layer of noodles
   - Tomato sauce
   - Remainder of béchamel sauce
   - Parmesan cheese sprinkled on top

7. Bake at 350° for 45 minutes. Remove and let rest 5 minutes before cutting and serving.

Sesame-Maple Roasted Tofu

MAKES: 6 servings

PREP. TIME: 15 minutes

BAKING TIME: 40 minutes

Serve over Asian (udon) noodles and even tofu-suspicious guests will agree this is a tasty dish.

INGREDIENTS:

- 14-oz. block extra-firm tofu, rinsed, patted dry and cut into 1" cubes
- 1 medium red onion, sliced
- 2 tsp. canola oil
- 2 tsp. toasted sesame oil
- ¼ tsp. salt
- ¼ tsp. freshly ground black pepper
- 1 Tbsp. tahini (ground sesame paste)
- 1 Tbsp. soy sauce (may be reduced-sodium)
- 2 tsp. pure maple syrup
- 1 tsp. cider vinegar
- 3 cups snap peas, trimmed (or 2 cups frozen peas)
- 1 Tbsp. sesame seeds

1. Toss the tofu cubes, onion, canola and sesame oils, salt, and pepper in large bowl. Spread on a rimmed baking sheet and roast in 450° oven until tofu is lightly golden on top and onions are browning in spots, 15–20 minutes.

2. Whisk tahini, soy sauce, maple syrup, and vinegar in a small dish until combined.

3. Remove tofu from the oven, add peas, and drizzle with the maple sauce; stir to combine.

4. Return to oven and continue roasting until the peas are crisp-tender, 8–12 minutes.

5. Sprinkle with sesame seeds. Serve hot.

Vegetarian Indian Stew

MAKES: 6 servings

PREP. TIME: 15 minutes

COOKING TIME: 30 minutes

INGREDIENTS:

2 Tbsp. olive oil

1 large onion, sliced

1 Tbsp. minced garlic

2 small green chilies, seeded and sliced (or half 4-oz. can green chilies)

1 tsp. ground cumin

2 tsp. curry powder

1 tsp. ground turmeric

4 cups vegetable stock

1 cup red lentils, rinsed and drained

3 large tomatoes, coarsely chopped

2 potatoes, in bite-size pieces

1 tsp. brown sugar

¼ cup chopped cilantro

¼ cup chopped fresh mint

1 cup canned, drained garbanzo beans

1 large ripe mango, peeled and cubed (fresh, frozen or canned)

1. In a large pot over medium heat, sauté onions in olive oil until soft, about 7 minutes. Add garlic, green chilies, cumin, curry powder, and turmeric. Reduce heat to medium-low and cook about 2 minutes, stirring constantly, to bring out flavor of spices.

2. Add stock and lentils; bring to a boil and simmer, covered, for 10 minutes.

3. Add tomatoes, potatoes, sugar, and half the cilantro and mint. Reduce heat and cook, covered, until potatoes are almost tender, about 15 minutes.

4. Stir in garbanzo beans; simmer, covered, about 6 minutes.

5. Stir in mango and simmer, covered, only until heated through, about 2 minutes.

6. Serve stew sprinkled with remaining cilantro and mint, and if desired, a dollop of yogurt.

This stew was a big hit when we made it for a young friend who was hosting a week-long class for builders at his under-construction home. The apprentices were learning to hand mix sand, clay, and straw to form blocks. The host needed to provide vegetarian meals for 15 hungry workers each day. Spouse Alice volunteered to prepare this hearty dish for a midday meal. The Oregonian instructor told her, "I have had classes all over the world, but nothing I have been served elsewhere can match this cuisine."

Roasted Red Pepper and Lentil Loaf

MAKES: 6 servings

PREP. TIME: 15 minutes

BAKING TIME: 30–35 minutes

STANDING TIME: 10 minutes

INGREDIENTS:

2 eggs

2 Tbsp. olive oil

2 Tbsp. water

15-oz. can lentils, drained and rinsed

½ cup finely chopped red onion

2 cups chopped baby spinach

8-oz. jar roasted red pepper, cut in ½" pieces

½ cup feta cheese (2 oz.)

6-oz. package falafel mix

1. In bowl, whisk together eggs, oil, and water. Mix in lentils, onion, spinach, and red pepper to combine. Fold in cheese.

2. Gradually add falafel mix and stir well to combine.

3. Transfer mixture to a rimmed 9" x 13" baking sheet lined with foil. Shape into a loaf, about 9" x 3 ½".

4. Bake at 375˚ for 30–35 minutes, until internal temperature registers 150˚. Remove from oven and let rest for 10 minutes before slicing.

Rice with Apples and Onions

MAKES: 6 servings

PREP. TIME: 15 minutes

COOKING: 30 minutes

INGREDIENTS:

6 apples of choice, unpeeled but sliced

¼ cup water

¼ cup honey *or* pure maple syrup

3 large white sweet onions, sliced

1 Tbsp. olive oil

1 cup white rice

1 cup water

1. In pan, cook apples and water over medium heat until slightly soft, about 15 minutes; add sweetener near end of cooking.

2. In another pan, brown onions in oil over medium heat, stirring until golden. Add rice and water. Bring to a boil, reduce heat and simmer until liquid is gone, about 20 minutes. Mix well.

3. Pile rice on serving platter and border with apples.

4. Serve with cheese board and salad of choice.

POULTRY AND SEAFOOD

Baked Herb Turkey Breast

MAKES: 12 servings

PREP. TIME: 10 minutes

BAKING TIME: 2 hours

A slow oven bake produces a flavor-bursting breast using Joyce Eby's effortless recipe from Blessings for the Table: From the Laurelville Family.

INGREDIENTS:

¼ cup olive oil

3 cloves garlic, minced

1 tsp. dried rosemary, *or*
    2 tsp. fresh rosemary

1 turkey breast (5–6 lbs.)

1. In cup or bowl, mix oil, garlic, and rosemary.

2. Loosen skin of turkey breast and brush half of the oil mixture between meat and skin.

3. Bake at 325° for 1 hour, covered.

4. Uncover and bake 1 hour more, basting every 15 minutes with remaining oil mixture.

Tip: An oven thermometer enables more accurate baking time; temperature should reach 165 degrees Fahrenheit.

Aunt Stella's Overnight Chicken Casserole

MAKES: 8 servings

PREP. TIME: 20 minutes

RESTING TIME: overnight (optional)

BAKING TIME: 1 ½ hours

INGREDIENTS:

8–10 slices bread

4 cups chicken, cooked and chopped

2 12-oz. cans cream of mushroom soup

½ cup mayonnaise

8-oz. can sliced mushrooms, drained

8-oz. can sliced water chestnuts, drained

1 jar chopped pimento, *optional*

Cheddar cheese slices to cover 9" x 13" baking pan

4 eggs

2 cups milk

4 cups stuffing mix, or dry bread crumbs

½ cup butter, melted

Communities and churches often use anniversaries as impetus for a cookbook. The following chicken recipes are from such collections in my home state of Iowa. This dish and Chicken and Biscuits in Casserole are from Swedesburg Lutherans celebrating their centennial in 1966. Baked Chicken Loaf is from the 1982 cookbook commemorating the 25th anniversary of Washington Mennonite Church. Baked Chicken Royal comes from Midwest Old Settlers 1973 Souvenir Cook Book from Mt. Pleasant, Iowa.

1. Line a greased 9" x 13" pan with the bread. Cover with chicken.

2. Mix soup, mayonnaise, mushrooms, water chestnuts, and pimentos; pour mixture over chicken and cover with cheese.

3. Beat eggs and milk together and pour over the casserole.

4. Refrigerate overnight if desired, or bake immediately at 300° for 1 ½ hours.

5. Mix stuffing and melted butter. One hour into baking time, sprinkle over entire casserole, and return to oven for remainder of time.

Prepare Saturday night, set oven before church, and lunch is ready when you get home.

Baked Chicken Loaf

MAKES: 8—10 servings

PREP. TIME: 15 minutes

BAKING TIME: 45 minutes

INGREDIENTS:

- 4 cups cooked chicken, cut up
- 2 cups bread crumbs
- 4 eggs, beaten
- ½ tsp. salt
- 4 ribs celery, chopped
- 2 cups chicken broth
- 1 cup crushed potato chips, or buttered bread crumbs

1. In bowl, mix all ingredients except potato chips. Place in greased 2 qt. baking dish.

2. Top with crushed chips or buttered crumbs.

3. Bake at 350° for 45 minutes.

Baked Chicken Royal

MAKES: 8–10 servings

PREP. TIME: 20 minutes

BAKING TIME: 30 minutes

INGREDIENTS:

1 stewing chicken (3–4 lbs)

4 eggs

6 Tbsp. butter

6 Tbsp. flour

1 qt. milk

½ tsp. salt

¼ tsp. black pepper

½ cup cracker crumbs

1. Cook chicken. When cool, debone and finely chop meat.

2. Hard boil eggs and peel when cooled. Chop the whites and crumble yolks.

3. To make gravy, melt butter in pan over medium heat. Stir in flour to make paste, then slowly add milk. Simmer, stirring constantly, until thickened. Add salt and pepper. Set aside to cool.

4. In greased 2 qt. casserole, begin with layer using ⅓ of gravy, then a layer using ½ of chicken, then ½ of the egg mixture. Repeat this, ending with gravy on top. Sprinkle cracker crumbs over all.

5. Bake at 350° for 30 minutes.

Oven-Fried Chicken Parmesan

MAKES: 4 servings
PREP. TIME: 20 minutes
BAKING TIME: 45 minutes

INGREDIENTS:

1 cup crushed herb
  stuffing, or coarse dry
  bread crumbs

⅔ cup grated Parmesan
  cheese

¼ cup chopped parsley

1 clove garlic, minced

1 frying chicken, cut up
  (2 ½–3 lbs.)

½ cup butter, melted

1. Combine stuffing crumbs, cheese, parsley, and garlic. If using bread crumbs, add ½ tsp. salt and ¼ tsp. black pepper.

2. Dip chicken in the butter, and roll in crumbs.

3. Place pieces, skin side up, so they do not touch, in a jelly roll or shallow baking pan. Sprinkle with any remaining butter and crumbs.

4. Bake at 375° for 45 minutes or until tender (it is not necessary to turn the chicken).

Michigan Salmon Chowder

MAKES: 8 servings

PREP. TIME: 20 minutes

COOKING TIME: 45–60 minutes

INGREDIENTS:

1 onion, chopped

4 ribs celery, chopped

1 Tbsp. olive oil

Herbal seasonings of choice

½ cup white wine

½ lb. fresh salmon

2 potatoes with peel, chopped

16 oz. corn kernels, fresh *or* frozen

14-oz. can vegetable *or* chicken broth

2 cups water

2 Tbsp. flour

1 cup milk

dry sherry, *optional*

1. In Dutch oven, sauté onion and celery in oil with seasonings. Add wine and salmon. Steam until salmon is flaky (about 5 minutes).

2. Add potatoes, corn, and broth. Over medium heat, simmer 30–40 minutes, adding water to taste.

3. Just before serving, whisk flour into milk, add to chowder, and bring to boil while stirring, but do not prolong cooking.

4. If you wish, you may top each bowl with 1 oz. dry sherry before serving.

Chicken and Biscuits in Casserole

MAKES: 8–10 servings

PREP. TIME: 30 minutes

BAKING TIME: 30 minutes

INGREDIENTS:

GRAVY:

¼ cup flour

½ cup milk

1 qt. chicken broth

4 cups chicken, cooked and
 cut up

BISCUITS:

½ tsp. salt

1 Tbsp. baking powder

2 cups flour

½ cup butter, at room
 temperature

1 egg

½ cup milk

1. In jar with tight lid, shake flour and milk together until smooth.

2. Stir flour mixture into hot broth. Simmer, stirring constantly, until mixture thickens.

3. Add boned chicken and place mixture in greased 9" x 13" baking dish.

1. Add salt and baking powder to flour; cut butter into flour mixture, or pulse in food processor.

2. Beat egg and milk together. Mix with flour to make a ball of soft dough.

3. On floured surface, roll dough to about ¼" thickness. Cut into 2" circles (makes 12–15). Place biscuits on top of chicken casserole.

4. Bake at 400˚ for 30 minutes.

Pecan Crunch Salmon Bake

MAKES: 4 servings

PREP. TIME: 15 minutes

BAKING TIME: 15 minutes

After being given a fresh catch from a fisher friend I responded: "It was so thoughtful for you to remember my love for salmon. In return I send along, as you requested, my recipes (recognizing I prepare by instinct rather than by following the letter, like playing the piano by ear). I used the first package of your catch for a chowder and the second for a baked entree served with home-frozen green beans, corn, and Harvard beets accompanied by Australian Pinot Grigio white wine."

INGREDIENTS:

2 Tbsp. butter, melted

2 Tbsp. honey

2 Tbsp. Dijon mustard

⅓ cup fresh bread crumbs

⅓ cup chopped pecans

⅓ cup finely chopped fresh parsley

4 6-oz. salmon filets

Freshly ground coarse sea salt

Freshly ground black pepper

1. In small bowl, mix butter, honey, and mustard.

2. In another bowl, combine bread crumbs, pecans, and parsley.

3. Season salmon filets on both sides with salt and pepper, and place on broiling pan or baking sheet. (I use parchment paper to make cleanup easier.) Brush tops with the mustard mixture, then pat the pecan mixture as thickly as you can on each filet.

4. Bake at 400° for 10–15 minutes depending on filet thickness. (When I prepared this recently, I cooked the filets for 12 minutes and they were acclaimed "the best salmon I have ever eaten in the Midwest.")

5. Serve with lemon wedges.

Bay Scallops Thai-Style

MAKES: 6 servings

PREP. TIME: 5 minutes

COOKING TIME: 12–15 minutes

An easy to prepare one-dish entrée with distinctive guest-pleasing flavor. Its simplicity enables me to share lunch or supper after my quick preparation in the kitchen of a convalescing friend, or deliver as a carryout from my home.

INGREDIENTS:

- 7 oz. pasta of choice
- 12 oz. frozen vegetable of choice
- 12 oz. frozen bay scallops
- ½ cup crunchy natural peanut butter
- ¼ cup reduced-sodium soy sauce
- ¼ cup rice vinegar
- 1 Tbsp. hot chili-garlic sauce

1. Cook pasta as directed on package; during last five minutes of cooking, add vegetables and scallops (scallops should turn white and opaque).

2. Meanwhile mix other ingredients until smooth.

3. Drain pasta mixture and return to pan; toss with sauce and serve immediately.

Scallop and Sugar Snap Stir-Fry

MAKES: 4 servings

PREPARATION AND COOKING TIME: 30 minutes

INGREDIENTS:

½ cup chicken broth

2 Tbsp. rice wine

1 Tbsp. cornstarch

2 Tbsp. canola oil

2 green onions, thinly sliced

1 clove garlic, minced

¼ tsp. hot chili flakes

12-oz. sea scallops, rinsed, patted dry, and halved

12-oz. package sugar snap peas, partially thawed

½ cup slivered fresh basil leaves

1. In glass measure, whisk broth, rice wine, and cornstarch until well blended.

2. Over medium-high heat, pour oil into 12″ nonstick pan. Stir in onions, garlic, and chili flakes and fry about a minute. Add scallops, stirring occasionally until mostly opaque (about 2 minutes).

3. Stir in sugar snap peas and cook a minute longer. Pour in broth mixture, stirring until sauce is thick and glossy (2–3 more minutes).

4. Stir in half the basil, pour into serving bowl, and sprinkle with remaining basil.

5. Serve with couscous or brown rice.

BEEF, LAMB, AND PORK

Beer-Braised Short Ribs

For a slow cooker (ideal size: 5 qt.)

MAKES: 6 servings

PREP. TIME: 15 minutes

COOKING TIME: 4 hours

Colcannon or polenta topped with this mix of beer and beef equals a hearty winter supper.

INGREDIENTS:

2 lbs. boneless beef short ribs

2 tsp. sea salt

2 tsp. black pepper

1 Tbsp. canola oil

2 12-oz. cans Guinness Draught

2 cups beef broth

2 carrots, cut in 2" chunks

2 parsnips, cut in 1 ½" chunks

2 onions, peeled and quartered

2 celery ribs, cut in 1 ½" chunks

8 cloves garlic, peeled

1 Tbsp. brown sugar

½ cup dried cranberries *or* raisins

2 bay leaves

1. Season ribs with salt and pepper; add oil to large skillet over high heat. When oil is hot, add ribs, turning occasionally until browned, about 10 minutes. Transfer to slow cooker on high.

2. Deglaze hot skillet by pouring in beer and scraping up any brown bits; pour beer with bits over ribs.

3. Add remaining ingredients, and cook 4 hours.

4. Serve over colcannon (see *recipe in Celtic St Patrick Day lunch menu*) or polenta (whisk ¾ cup cornmeal into 4 cups simmering water; stir until thick, about 15 minutes). Top with *gremolata* (½ cup chopped fresh parsley, 1 minced clove garlic, zest of 1 orange and 1 lemon).

Classic Meatloaf

MAKES: 12 servings (6 cups)

PREP. TIME: 15 minutes

COOKING TIME: 1 hour

Meatloaf defies precision either in recipe or ingredients in my kitchen. I learned to make meatloaf by imitating my mother. She maintained that a quality loaf began with equal parts of farm-butchered pork and beef. After that it was instinct and intuition. What follows is the ideal recipe that's in my head when I set forth to make meatloaf.

INGREDIENTS:

- 1 ½ lbs. 90%-lean ground sirloin
- 1 ½ lbs. whole-hog sausage
- 4 oz. saltines (1 sleeve), finely crushed
- 2 eggs
- ½ cup finely chopped onion
- ¾ cup tomato, or vegetable, juice
- 1 Tbsp. dry oregano
- 1 Tbsp. Worcestershire sauce
- ½ cup finely chopped fresh parsley
- 2 tsp. freshly ground black pepper
- 2 Tbsp. Dijon mustard
- 2 Tbsp. catsup

1. With washed hands, combine meats in mixing bowl, then mix in saltines. Add eggs and mix thoroughly before adding remaining ingredients, except mustard and catsup.

2. Form two equal loaves and place on sprayed baking sheet; with a teaspoon handle, trace an indentation lengthwise through the middle of each loaf. Combine mustard and catsup, and pour into indentation.

3. Bake at 375° for 55 minutes.

Variations: Substitute ground turkey or chicken (half white, half dark meat), 1 cup quick oats instead of the saltines, and vary the spices.

Buffalo Red-Eye Stew

MAKES: 16 (1-cup) servings

PREP. TIME: 20 minutes

COOKING TIME: 45 minutes

Straight from the chuckwagon, this recipe comes from Denver's Buckhorn, a National Historic Landmark serving Old West fare since 1893.

INGREDIENTS:

- 4 potatoes, cut into 1" cubes
- 4 oz. butter
- 2 lbs. buffalo sirloin, cut in 1" cubes
- ½ cup chopped yellow onion
- 1 tsp. white pepper
- 1 tsp. thyme leaf
- 1 tsp. rosemary
- 2 tsp. basil
- 2 tsp. salt
- 1 Tbsp. granulated garlic
- 1 cup all-purpose flour
- 28-oz. can diced tomatoes
- ½ cup bourbon
- ½ cup strong coffee
- 2 cups water
- 1 Tbsp. Worcestershire sauce
- 6 bread bowls, optional

1. In saucepan, cover potatoes with water and bring to boil; simmer 10 minutes over medium heat (until about half done).

2. In another saucepan, melt butter over medium heat. Sauté sirloin, onion, pepper, thyme, rosemary, basil, salt, and garlic; simmer 3–5 minutes. Add flour and mix well. Cook 5 minutes.

3. Stir tomatoes into buffalo mixture and simmer 5 minutes. Drain potatoes and add bourbon, coffee, water and Worcestershire sauce. Return to boil; reduce heat and simmer about 30 minutes, or until buffalo is tender.

4. Divide between 6 soup bowls or bread bowls.

Balsamic Honey-Glazed Lamb Chops

MAKES: 6 servings

PREP. TIME: 20 minutes

COOKING TIME: 20 minutes

INGREDIENTS:

6 lamb chops

1 Tbsp. olive oil

1 tsp. dried thyme leaves

1 tsp. coarse black pepper

1 tsp. salt

⅓ cup balsamic vinegar

⅓ cup honey

⅓ cup sweet wine of choice

3 pears *or* apples, cored, sliced, and quartered

1. Brush lamb chops with oil and sprinkle with thyme, pepper, and salt. In large skillet over medium heat, cook chops for 5 minutes on each side.

2. In another skillet over medium heat, bring vinegar, honey, and wine to boil. Add fruit to bubbling mixture, turning to coat and cook until glazed and tender.

3. Place browned chops into fruit skillet. Turn every minute to glaze until desired doneness. Serve with couscous.

Pork Stir-Fry with Mixed Vegetables

MAKES: 4 servings

PREP. TIME: 10 minutes

STANDING TIME: 10 minutes

COOKING TIME: 10 minutes

INGREDIENTS:

1 Tbsp. balsamic vinegar

1 Tbsp. light soy sauce

1 Tbsp. sesame oil with ginger

1 tsp. garlic granules

1 lb. pork tenderloin, cut into 1" cubes

16-oz package frozen stir-fry Asian vegetables, thawed

1. In bowl, mix vinegar, soy sauce, oil, and garlic. Add tenderloin and marinate 10 minutes.

2. In skillet on medium high, stir-fry marinated meat 3 minutes, reserving any liquid in bowl.

3. Stir in vegetables, add reserved liquid, cover and cook for 3 minutes.

4. Serve hot with cooked grain of choice.

Autumn Pork Stew

MAKES: 6 servings

PREP. TIME: 15 minutes

COOKING TIME: 40 minutes

INGREDIENTS:

2 Tbsp. canola oil

1 onion, peeled and chopped

1 red bell pepper, chopped

1 clove garlic, peeled and chopped

1 ½ lbs. boneless pork loin, cut into 1" cubes

14-oz can chicken broth

1 cup dry white wine

1 tsp. dried thyme

1 tsp. dried rosemary

2 bay leaves

2 cups butternut squash, cut into 1 ½" cubes

2 cups carrots, sliced in ¾" slices

4 oz. fresh mushrooms, sliced

18 dried apricots

1 Granny Smith apple, cored and sliced

1. In Dutch oven over medium heat, sauté onion, pepper, and garlic in oil. Add pork and stir until no longer pink (5–7 minutes).

2. Add broth, wine, and herbs. Cover and simmer 10 minutes.

3. Add squash and carrots. Cover and simmer 10 minutes.

4. Add mushrooms, apricots, and apple. Cover and simmer 10 more minutes.

5. Serve warm, with or without rice.

Indiana Lamb Burgers with Yogurt-Mint Sauce

MAKES: 8 servings

PREP. TIME: 15 minutes

COOKING TIME: 10 minutes

INGREDIENTS:

2 lbs. ground lamb (locally grown preferred!)

¾ cup hazelnuts, toasted

1 ½ tsp. ground pepper

1 tsp. lemon pepper

1 Tbsp. lemon zest

1 tsp. salt

SAUCE:

¾ cup plain Greek yogurt

3 Tbsp. chopped fresh mint

1 ½ Tbsp. fresh lemon juice

1. In bowl, mix lamb, nuts, peppers, zest, and salt. Form mixture into 8 patties.

2. Grill over medium heat or broil, about 3 minutes on each side.

3. Mix sauce ingredients and spread on toasted buns; add lamb patties. Serve.

Coffee-Crusted Beef Rib-Eye Roast

MAKES: 6–8 servings

PREP. TIME: 15 minutes

BAKING TIME: 2–3 hours

STANDING TIME: 15 minutes

INGREDIENTS:

4–6 lb. beef rib-eye roast

RUB:

1 Tbsp. finely ground coffee beans

1 Tbsp. dark brown sugar

1 tsp. coarsely ground salt

1 tsp. coarsely ground black pepper

SAUCE:

1 cup balsamic vinegar

4 oz. (1 stick) butter, at room temperature

1 Tbsp. all-purpose flour

1 cup beef broth

1. In bowl, combine rub ingredients; press into all sides of roast. Position roast with fat side up on rack in shallow pan in 350° oven. Place thermometer in center, not resting in fat. Remove when temperature reaches 135° (medium-rare) or 150° (medium).

2. Transfer to carving board; tent loosely with foil. Let stand 15 minutes. Skim fat from drippings and reserve.

3. In saucepan over medium heat, bring vinegar to boil and simmer until reduced to ¼ cup. In small bowl, mix flour and butter until smooth. Add drippings and broth to pan, and gradually whisk in butter mixture; bring to boil. Reduce heat; simmer 1 minute, stirring constantly. Keep warm to serve over meat after carved in slices.

Orchard Apple Pork Chops

MAKES: 4 servings

PREP. TIME: 10 minutes

COOKING TIME: 20 minutes

INGREDIENTS:

4 center-cut ¾"-thick pork chops, trimmed of extra fat

1 Tbsp. canola oil

Salt and pepper to taste

1 ½ cups hard apple cider, *divided*

¼ cup whole-grain Dijon mustard

⅓ cup golden raisins

2 apples of choice, cored and sliced

2 green onions, sliced

1 Tbsp. cornstarch

1. In large skillet over medium-high heat, brown chops in oil, about 2 minutes per side. Season with salt and pepper.

2. While chops are browning, combine 1 ¼ cups cider with mustard in a bowl. Pour over chops, cover and lower heat; cook 3 minutes.

3. Add raisins, apples, and onions; cook 3–5 minutes more. Remove chops to serving platter and tent with foil to keep warm.

4. In cup, combine ¼ cup cider with cornstarch; whisk this into cooking liquid in skillet. Cook until thick.

5. Pour sauce over chops and serve.

Eight decades as host and guest at home and away
1953–1962

Two years later, as a University of Iowa journalism student, I made another food discovery. When several mates asked me to go out for pizza pie, I wondered what kind of pie that was. Pizza wasn't familiar to a farm boy for whom Uncle's Vernon's vast dessert pie repertoire had never included the emerging Italian favorite doused with tomato sauce and cheese. With that discovery my taste buds and culinary efforts began an international journey beyond the boundaries of Alsatian-influenced midwestern Mennonite flavors.

My great grandmother, according to my slender dad, weighed 300 pounds. That was my excuse for tipping the scales at nearly 200 when I came home from college after my nineteenth annual angel food cake. Love of food, cooking as well as eating it, was genetic. As manager of the college Snack Shop I felt it only right that I sample the food I served, along with tasting any new candy variety offered by the wholesale distributor. The summer before I got married I decided my affection for food must take secondary place. Hard farm labor combined with a diet of cottage cheese, grapefruit, and grilled steaks lowered my weight to normal (for my body frame). It was an intentional action I never regretted.

Enroute to Farm on the Hill in the Pocono Mountains, our August 1956 honeymoon Sunday lunch at The Country House (New Kingston, Pennsylvania) was noted as an all you care to eat country dinner for $2.95: savory and abundant. At Farm on the Hill, our honeymoon hideout in the Poconos, I tasted honeydew melon for the first time.

As house guests of Merrill and Boots Raber on our first visit to California in 1961 we dined at a Belgian restaurant in Hollywood. My entrée choice at Villa Frascati was canard a l'orange (roast Long Island duckling with orange sauce and wild rice) beginning with pâté maison and salad nicoise ending with mousse chocolat.

SIDES

BREADS

Hearty Irish Soda Bread

MAKES: 1 loaf, about 12 servings

PREP. TIME: 10 minutes

STANDING TIME: 5 minutes

BAKING TIME: 45 minutes

INGREDIENTS:

4 cups all-purpose flour, or substitute up to 2 cups whole wheat

1 tsp. salt

¾ tsp. baking soda

¾ tsp. baking powder

1 ½ cup buttermilk or plain yogurt

½ cup currants *or* raisins, *optional*

1. Combine flour, salt, baking soda, and baking powder.

2. Add buttermilk or yogurt to make a soft but not too sticky dough. (If using currants or raisins, add them just before stirring ingredients together.)

3. Knead about 3 minutes, then let dough rest 3–5 minutes.

4. Shape into round loaf on a greased baking sheet.

5. Slash an X on top of the loaf with a sharp knife.

6. Bake at 375° about 45 minutes, until loaf is golden brown and sounds hollow when bottom is tapped.

Tip: Soda bread should be eaten within 24 hours.

Easy 7-Grain Bread

MAKES: 2 loaves of 16 slices

PREP. TIME: 15 minutes

STANDING TIME: 30–45 minutes

BAKING TIME: 45 minutes

From Canadian friends I learned that 7-grain cereal is not only an oatmeal alternative for warm winter breakfasts, but can be transformed without kneading into a hearty home loaf.

INGREDIENTS:

1 ½ cups boiling water

1 cup 7-grain cereal

2 Tbsp. dry yeast

½ cup warm water

6 Tbsp. oil

½ cup honey

2 eggs, beaten

3 ½ cups whole wheat flour

2 cups all-purpose flour

1. In large mixing bowl, pour boiling water over cereal and stir until smooth; let cool.

2. In measuring cup, dissolve yeast in warm water; add to cereal when cereal is lukewarm.

3. Add oil, honey, eggs, and whole wheat flour to cereal; beat vigorously for 2 ½ minutes.

4. Work in all-purpose flour for a couple additional minutes.

5. Divide dough in half and spread into two greased 9" x 5" loaf pans; let rise until double.

6. Bake at 375° for 45 minutes.

7. Turn out to cool on rack.

Carrot-Oatmeal Muffins

MAKES: 12 muffins

PREP. TIME: 10 minutes

BAKING TIME: 20 minutes

A 25-year-old recipe combining carrots and oatmeal, even before cutting cholesterol concerned us.

INGREDIENTS:

½ cup all-purpose flour

½ cup whole wheat flour

2 tsp. baking powder

½ tsp. baking soda

½ tsp. salt

1 Tbsp. cinnamon

⅓ cup brown sugar

1 cup milk

1 egg, beaten

¼ cup butter, melted

1 cup shredded carrots

1 cup quick oats

1. In large mixing bowl, combine flours, baking powder, baking soda, and salt.
2. Mix in cinnamon, brown sugar, milk, egg, and butter.
3. Add carrots and oats, mixing just enough to combine.
4. Spoon into well-greased 12-muffin tin, making each muffin cup about ⅔ full.
5. Bake at 375° for about 20 minutes (may take longer).
6. Loosen with spatula after cooling for several minutes.

Rhubarb Muffins

MAKES: 12 muffins

PREP. TIME: 10 minutes

BAKING TIME: 30 minutes

This recipe links one of my favorite spring garden perennials with a favorite way of making a quick bread. It is adapted from the Michigan kitchen of Lovina Eicher, known to many South Bend (Indiana) Tribune readers as The Amish Cook.

INGREDIENTS:

2 cups all-purpose flour

1 cup sugar

2 tsp. baking powder

½ tsp. salt

1 egg

1 cup milk

⅓ cup oil

1 cup chopped rhubarb, fresh or frozen

¼ cup sugar

1. Combine flour, sugar, baking powder, and salt in a bowl.

2. In another bowl, beat together the egg, milk, and oil. Mix into dry ingredients, stirring until just moistened. Fold in rhubarb.

3. Fill well-greased muffin pan, each cup ¾ full; sprinkle with sugar.

4. Bake at 350° for 25–30 minutes, or until a toothpick comes out clean.

5. Loosen muffins from pan, cool 5 minutes, and serve warm with or without butter.

Guinness Beer Bread

MAKES: 1 loaf

PREP. TIME: 10 minutes

BAKING TIME: 70 minutes

For non-beer lovers who still crave the nourishment of the B vitamins in Ireland's favorite drink, this recipe provides an easy and tasty way to partake of the healthy elements.

INGREDIENTS:

4 cups all-purpose flour, *or* 1 cup can be whole wheat

2 Tbsp. baking powder

1 tsp. salt

¼ cup sugar

12 oz. Guinness "Draught" beer

2 eggs, slightly beaten

1. Combine flour, baking powder, salt, and sugar.
2. Add beer and eggs, stirring just until batter is blended.
3. Pour into greased 9″ x 5″ loaf pan.
4. Bake at 375° for 60–70 minutes.
5. Remove from pan and cool.

Tip: Can be baked in 2 smaller loaf pans; reduce baking time to 45 minutes.

Welsh Cakes

MAKES: 12 cakes (6 servings)

PREP. TIME: 10 minutes

COOKING TIME: 18 minutes

Wales quickly became a favorite family vacation spot when we stopped en route to our first missionary term in West Africa. Bed and breakfast sometimes included this almost familiar version of pancakes, which always warmed the hearts and stomachs of our two primary schoolers.

INGREDIENTS:

2 cups all-purpose flour

½ tsp. baking powder

⅛ tsp. salt

½ cup (one stick) butter

⅓ cup sugar

¼ tsp. spice of choice

⅓ cup raisins or currants

1 egg, beaten

1 Tbsp. milk

1. Mix together flour, baking powder and salt, cut in butter.
2. Add sugar, spice and raisins.
3. Stir in the egg and milk.
4. On floured surface, roll out to ½" thick. Cut into 2 ½" rounds (12–15 cakes).
5. Cook on griddle glazed with butter, over low to medium heat, 3 minutes per side.
6. Serve warm with butter.

Crispy Cornmeal Waffles

MAKES: 12–16 servings

PREP. TIME: 15 minutes

BAKING TIME: as desired, to offer hot waffles as needed

Waffles are a hospitality tradition in Alice's family, appropriately served for breakfast, lunch, or supper. Although traditionally enjoyed with slathers of real butter and genuine maple syrup, fresh waffles may also be topped with fruits of all varieties (fresh, frozen, or canned); creamed chicken, tuna, or turkey; yogurt—and to end, a large scoop of ice cream.

INGREDIENTS:

2 eggs, separated

1 ¾ c. milk

1 cup cornmeal

1 cup all-purpose flour

2 Tbsp. sugar, optional

1 Tbsp. baking powder

1 tsp. salt

5 Tbsp. oil

1. Beat egg whites until slightly stiff; set aside.

2. Mix egg yolks with milk, cornmeal, flour, sugar, baking powder, and salt, then gradually add oil.

3. Fold in beaten egg whites.

4. Bake in hot waffle iron until lightly browned and crisp. Serve warm.

Bara Brith (Welsh Speckled Bread)

MAKES: 16 servings

PREP. TIME: 30 minutes

STANDING TIME: 12 hours

BAKING TIME: 1 hour

Another traditional bread from Wales that freezes well. Handy for serving with a hot drink to unexpected guests.

INGREDIENTS:

1 lb. mixed dried fruit, chopped if needed

1 ¼ cups freshly brewed strong tea

½ cup brown sugar

2 cups all-purpose flour

1 cup whole wheat flour

1 Tbsp. + 1 tsp. baking powder

¼ tsp. salt

2 tsp. ground cinnamon

½ tsp. ground cloves

1 egg, beaten

3 Tbsp. orange marmalade

1. Place dried fruit in large bowl and cover with tea. Add brown sugar and mix well. Cover and let stand at room temperature 12 hours or overnight.

2. Combine dry ingredients, then add to fruit mixture with blended egg and marmalade.

3. Spoon dough into 9″ x 5″ greased loaf pan, or two smaller pans.

4. Bake at 350° about 1 hour, or until bread is brown and crusty and toothpick inserted near center comes out clean. Reduce time to 45 minutes for smaller loaves.

5. Cool, wrap tightly in plastic wrap, and store at room temperature for several days. Refrigerate or freeze for longer keeping.

Mother's Spanish Coffee Cake

MAKES: 16 servings

PREP. TIME: 15 minutes

BAKING TIME: 30 minutes

Although not a world traveler, Mother enjoyed trying and tasting new recipes. She and Dad happily accompanied their missionary son on a mid-term holiday from assignment in West Africa to the cooler temperatures of Spain's Canary Islands. After her death, I was pleasantly surprised to find this recipe in her collection.

INGREDIENTS:

¾ cup oil

¾ cup sugar

1 cup brown sugar

2 ½ cups all-purpose flour

½ tsp. salt

2 ½ tsp. cinnamon, divided

½ cup chopped walnuts

1 cup buttermilk

1 tsp. baking soda

1 egg

1 cup confectioners sugar

1 Tbsp. cream

1 tsp. vanilla.

1. Mix together oil, sugars, flour, salt, and ½ tsp. cinnamon.

2. Take out ¾ cup of this mixture and add to it the nuts and 2 tsp. cinnamon. Set this aside for topping.

3. To remaining mixture, add buttermilk, soda, and egg. Mix well.

4. Pour into greased 9" x 13" baking pan. Sprinkle with topping.

5. Bake at 350° about 30 minutes.

6. Meanwhile, make frosting by mixing confectioners sugar, cream, and vanilla.

7. Frost coffee cake while still warm.

BEVERAGES

Holiday Cordials

INGREDIENTS:

COFFEE CORDIAL NO. 1

5 cups sugar

8 cups water

1 cup instant espresso powder

3 cups vodka

¼ cup vanilla extract

1. Combine sugar and water in saucepan, bring to boil, and simmer until sugar is dissolved, stirring occasionally. Remove from heat and stir in espresso powder until dissolved. Cool to room temperature.

2. Stir in vodka and vanilla.

3. Bottle and store in dark place for 8–12 weeks before using.

During a retirement residential year in Mile-High City, I took advantage of lifelong learning opportunities. On a December Saturday at Denver Public Library, Chef Jorge de la Torre, dean of culinary education at Johnson & Wales University, demonstrated recipes for winter holiday cordials. These economical liqueurs also make unique hostess gifts; Coffee Cordial No. 2 is the recipe I used one year. (Remember: make them in early October if you want to use them during the Christmas season.)

COFFEE CORDIAL NO. 2

¼ cup instant espresso powder

2 ½ cups brown sugar

1 cup water

¼ cup whole coffee beans of choice

3 cups brandy

1 Tbsp. vanilla extract

1. Combine espresso powder, brown sugar, and water in medium-size pan over medium heat; stir occasionally until mixture comes to boil. Lower heat and simmer for 5 minutes. Turn off heat and let cool in pan.

2. Put espresso-sugar syrup, coffee beans, and brandy into glass container with tight lid. Stir well, close, and store in cool, dry place for 2 weeks. Stir occasionally.

3. Add vanilla, stir, and re-seal; let sit for 2 more weeks.

4. Strain through double layer of cheesecloth into easy pouring vessel; strain through two new layers of cheesecloth and pour into smaller bottles for gift-giving.

MINT CORDIAL

3 cups sugar

1 ½ cups water

3 cups vodka

1 Tbsp. mint extract

1. Combine sugar and water in saucepan, bring to boil and simmer until sugar is dissolved, stirring occasionally. Remove from heat and cool to room temperature.

2. Stir in vodka and mint.

3. Bottle and store in dark place for 8–12 weeks before using.

Hot Ciders

INGREDIENTS:

HOLIDAY SPICED CIDER

2 cinnamon sticks

1 Tbsp. whole allspice

1 tsp. whole cloves

2 quarts fresh apple cider

1 quart cran-apple juice

½ cup brown sugar

1 quart boiling water

4 breakfast tea bags

1. Place cinnamon sticks, allspice, and cloves on two layers of cheesecloth. Bring up corners of cloth to form a bundle, and tie with a string to make spice bag.

2. Combine cider and cran-apple juice in slow cooker and stir in brown sugar.

3. Immerse tea bags in boiling water for 3 minutes, remove bags, and add tea to cooker.

4. Add spice bag to cooker.

5. Cook on low at least 3 hours before serving.

Apples are an autumn staple in the Midwest. Freshly pressed cider was a childhood favorite—long before I ever tasted Coke. Cider continues to be my seasonal beverage of choice, often served warm on a crisp November Sunday. I usually use a slow cooker, convenient for both preparation and serving. The following recipes may be modified at cook's discretion for the entertaining occasion. While fresh cider is preferable, frozen or canned may be used; alcohol additions are optional.

CIDER-CRANBERRY HOT TODDY

6 cups fresh apple cider

1 cup cranberry juice

½ cup brown sugar

½ cup tequila

½ cup triple sec

½ cup rum

1. Combine cider, cranberry juice, and brown sugar, and warm slowly in slow cooker or saucepan for at least 30 minutes.
2. Add liquor and warm another 30 minutes before serving.

APRICOT CIDER MUG

1 oz. apricot brandy

8 oz. heated fresh apple cider

Sprinkle of nutmeg

1. Put brandy in heated mug.
2. Add hot cider; sprinkle with nutmeg and serve to order.

Grandma Roth's Grape Juice

PREP. TIME: 15 minutes

COOKING TIME: 1 ½ hours

STANDING TIME: 2 hours

Along with fellow scholars in single room Stringtown School, I looked forward to the surprise announcement around May Day of the annual spring flower hunt in the Graber timber. Indoor classes suspended, the 15 students ranging from grades one to eight spent an afternoon discovering and identifying the flowers of the forest. Our last stop was always refreshment at the Graber farm where thirst was quenched with home-canned grape juice and soda crackers. This recipe comes from Uncle Vernon's recollection of Grandma's method for preserving Concord grapes.

INGREDIENTS:

10 lbs. grapes, removed from stem and washed

2 quarts boiling water

4 cups sugar (I use 3)

1. Simmer grapes in large saucepan about 1 ¼ hours. When skins and pulp separate, boil vigorously for 5 minutes.

2. Remove from heat and pour into a cloth-lined drainer; drain at least 2 hours.

3. Return to saucepan, add sugar, and boil an additional 5 minutes.

4. Pour into heated canning jars and seal, or into containers for freezing.

Celtic Citrus Squash

MAKES: 16 servings

PREP. TIME: 15 minutes

BAKING TIME: 30 minutes

Squash, the beverage not the vegetable, was developed in the British Isles as an inexpensive household alternative to beer and wine. The concentrate is easy to make in the home kitchen, easy to store, and easy to serve. The drink was popular during our family sojourn in the tropics, where citrus was plentiful year-round.

INGREDIENTS:

3 large ripe lemons

3 large ripe oranges

3 lbs. sugar

2 oz. citric acid

3 pints boiling water

1. Squeeze lemons and oranges, mince peel, and add sugar and citric acid.

2. Pour boiling water over fruit mix; leave 12 hours, stirring every 3 hours.

3. Strain and bottle. Keeps 6 weeks refrigerated.

4. Serve as desired, mixing 1 part concentrate with 4 parts water (more or less depending on preference).

Minty Lemon Tea

INGREDIENTS:

4 quarts boiling water, divided

2 cups fresh mint tea leaves, washed

4 breakfast tea bags

2 large ripe lemons

1. Pour 3 quarts boiling water over mint leaves in glass jar.
2. Pour 1 quart boiling water over tea bags in another container; remove bags after 3 minutes and add breakfast tea to mint tea.
3. Refrigerate 3–6 hours.
4. Juice and zest lemons and add to tea. Serve over ice.

Enjoying Wine

Wine puts life into anyone who drinks in moderation.
What is life to somebody deprived of wine?
Was it not created to bring joy to the heart?
—Sirach 31:27

I took my first wine course at the Western Wine Institute for Neophyte Oenophiles in Denver. Here I learned a new round of ABCs to help me appreciate linking good food and good drink.

Acidity: a refreshing quality that gives wine a crisp taste thus enhancing compatibility with food.
Balanced: acid, sugar, and fruit complement each other and taste good.
Complex: a wine with flavor levels showing different qualities in nose and taste with each sip.
Dry: a wine with little residual sugar.
Finish: tastes left in the mouth after swallowing; can be long, short, lovely, lousy.
Varietal: the name of the grape.
Vintage: the year harvested.

While not a wine connoisseur, I enjoy serving and drinking wines with food. All I need to know I can quickly learn from www.winespectator.com.

CHUTNEYS, RELISHES, AND SAUCES

Rhubarb Chutney

MAKES: 1 cup

PREP. TIME: 15 minutes

COOKING TIME: 10 minutes

INGREDIENTS:

1 shallot, finely chopped

1 Tbsp. raisins

2 Tbsp. white wine vinegar

¼ cup brown sugar

½ tsp. nutmeg

½ cinnamon stick

1 ½ cup rhubarb, sliced in 1" pieces

1. In saucepan, sauté shallot, raisins, vinegar, brown sugar, nutmeg, and cinnamon. Simmer 5 minutes.

2. Add rhubarb and cook 5 minutes more; remove cinnamon stick.

3. Serve warm or cold to accompany meat dishes.

Homestead Fruit Dressing

MAKES: 12 servings

PREP. TIME: 10 minutes

BAKING TIME: 30 minutes

My kitchen credits the no longer existent Homestead Inn, just off the Turnpike in central Ohio, with this dish that enhances almost anything it is served with.

INGREDIENTS:

16-oz. can sliced yellow cling peaches

16-oz. can sliced pears

16-oz. can pineapple chunks

16-oz. can apricot halves

⅓ cup raisins

⅓ cup walnuts

¾ cup brown sugar, divided

1 tsp. vanilla

½ lb. melted butter

5 slices white bread, toasted

1. Drain peaches, pears, and pineapple in a colander. Drain apricots and keep separate from other fruit. Put all fruit, except apricots, in a large bowl.

2. Add raisins, walnuts, ½ cup of the brown sugar, and vanilla. Mix lightly.

3. Pour into 9″ x 13″ baking pan, and arrange apricots evenly on top.

4. Cut toasted bread slices into ½″ squares and place on top. Pour melted butter and remainder of brown sugar over entire mixture.

5. Bake at 350˚ for 30 minutes. Serve warm.

Apricot and Raisin Chutney

MAKES: 1 cup

PREP. TIME: 20 minutes

INGREDIENTS:

½ cup dried apricots

½ cup raisins

½ cup boiling water

2 Tbsp. fresh lime juice

2 Tbsp. peach or apricot schnapps, *optional*

¼ tsp. cayenne pepper

1. In bowl, soak apricots and raisins in boiling water for 15 minutes.
2. Transfer to blender or food processor; add remaining ingredients and blend until smooth.
3. Cover and refrigerate until used.

Citrus Chutney

MAKES: 2 ½ cups

PREP. TIME: 15 minutes

STANDING TIME: 30 minutes

COOKING TIME: 30 minutes

INGREDIENTS:

⅓ cup white raisins

¼ cup triple sec

1 cup fresh grapefruit sections

1 cup fresh orange sections

½ cup finely diced red onion

2 Tbsp. white balsamic vinegar

2 Tbsp. brown sugar

1. Marinate raisins in triple sec for 30 minutes.
2. Combine all ingredients in saucepan, bring to boil, and simmer 20–30 minutes.
3. Serve warm or cold.

Hawkeye Corn Relish

MAKES: 6–8 servings

PREP. TIME: 10 minutes

STANDING TIME: 6 hours

My home state of Iowa holds the world's record for the tallest corn stalk and continues to be a top corn grower. Corn is a continuing staple in my kitchen. This relish can be put together quickly—it goes especially well with any broiled fish dish.

INGREDIENTS:

2 cups cooked corn kernels, fresh, frozen, *or* canned

1 cup finely chopped celery

½ cup finely chopped green onions

1 tsp. Dijon mustard

1 tsp. Worcestershire sauce

2 Tbsp. white vinegar

1. Combine all ingredients in bowl; mix well and cover tightly with plastic wrap.

2. Refrigerate 6 hours before serving.

Crunchy Pineapple Relish

MAKES: 1 ½ cups

PREP. TIME: 10 minutes

STANDING TIME: 30 minutes

INGREDIENTS:

1 cup finely diced fresh pineapple

1 cup finely diced, unpeeled English cucumber

2 Tbsp. finely diced red onion

2 Tbsp. fresh parsley, *and/or* fresh chives

1 tsp. fresh lime or lemon juice

1 Tbsp. seasoned rice vinegar

¼ tsp. freshly ground sea salt

¼ tsp. freshly ground black pepper

Mix all ingredients in small glass bowl and let stand, unrefrigerated, for at least 30 minutes, stirring several times.

Buckhorn Cinnamon Rum Sauce

MAKES: ¾ cup

PREP. TIME: 15 minutes

Buckhorn Exchange in Denver holds Colorado's second oldest liquor license. Chef Cesar Garcia is happy for customers to imitate the sauce he serves on his signature warm Dutch apple pie.

INGREDIENTS:

½ lb. salted butter

½ lb. confectioner's sugar

1 tsp. pure vanilla

1 tsp. cinnamon

1 Tbsp. dark rum

1. Combine all ingredients in bowl and mix on low until blended.
2. Continue mixing until volume doubles (about 3 minutes).
3. Serve immediately over a warmed dessert of cook's choice.

5-Bean Sweet-Sour Relish

MAKES: 6 cups

PREP. TIME: 15 minutes

INGREDIENTS:

¼ cup olive oil

2 Tbsp. seasoned rice vinegar

¼ tsp. dried thyme

2 Tbsp. honey

2 Tbsp Peppadew peppers

1 cup green beans, frozen

½ cup shelled edamame, frozen

15-oz. can wax beans, drained

15-oz. can kidney beans

15-oz. can black beans

1. In bowl with cover, whisk oil, vinegar, thyme, honey, and peppers.

2. Rinse frozen green beans and edamame under hot water and add to dressing.

3. Add three cans of beans. Mix well and cover to refrigerate.

4. Serve as a condiment to accent pasta and other dishes.

Tip: Peppadew peppers, produced in South Africa, are available in gourmet shops; any pepper of choice may be substituted, although the relish flavor will not be the same.

Gourmet Cranberry Rum Sauce

MAKES: 3 cups

PREP. TIME: 10 minutes

COOKING TIME: 20 minutes

INGREDIENTS:

½ cup sugar

½ cup dark brown sugar

¾ cup water

12-oz. package fresh cranberries

½ cup raisins

½ cup chopped walnuts

3 Tbsp. dark rum

1. In medium saucepan, combine sugars and water. Bring to boil over medium heat.

2. Add cranberries and return to boil. Gently boil for 10 minutes without stirring. Pour into glass mixing bowl.

3. Gently stir in raisins, walnuts, and rum. Cover with plastic wrap.

4. Cool to room temperature and refrigerate if not using immediately. Best served at room temperature.

VEGETABLES

Aunt Lucille's Scalloped Potatoes

MAKES: 8 servings

PREP. TIME: 30 minutes

BAKING TIME: 1 hour

INGREDIENTS:

2 Tbsp. butter

2 Tbsp. (generous) flour

3 cups hot milk

½ tsp. salt

¼ tsp. black pepper

1 tsp. dried onion

6 medium potatoes, sliced

½ cup shredded cheddar cheese

1. Make a white sauce by melting butter in small saucepan, adding flour and cooking for 3 minutes, stirring constantly. Add hot milk slowly, continuing to cook and stir until sauce is thickened and smooth (about 5 minutes). Add salt, pepper, and dried onion.

2. Put half the potatoes in a greased 2-quart casserole and cover with half the sauce. Repeat, using the remainder of potatoes and sauce.

3. Cover and bake at 350° for 1 hour or until done. Uncover, sprinkle with shredded cheese, and continue baking until cheese is melted.

Tip: You may partially boil the potatoes first to shorten the baking time. If white sauce seems too thick, add additional 2–4 Tbsp. milk.

Sweet-Sour Baked Beans

MAKES: 12 servings

PREP. TIME: 15 minutes

COOKING TIME: 4–6 hours in slow cooker or 1 hour in oven

Non-traditional recipe using four beans: white lima, green lima, kidney, and New England baked.

INGREDIENTS:

8 bacon slices

1 large onion, cut in rings

¾ cup brown sugar

1 Tbsp. prepared mustard

½ tsp. salt

½ cup cider vinegar

2 15-oz. cans white lima beans, drained

15-oz. can green lima beans, drained

15-oz. can kidney beans, drained

28-oz. can New England style baked beans, undrained

1. Fry bacon until crisp; pat off excess fat and crumble.

2. Pour off bacon drippings, leaving about 2 Tbsp. in skillet. Place onion in skillet, adding sugar, mustard, salt, and vinegar. Cook 20 minutes on low heat.

3. Combine the beans, and add onion mixture and bacon.

4. Cook in slow cooker for 4–6 hours on low, or 1 hour in oven at 350˚.

Aunt Lucille's Sauerkraut Salad

MAKES: 8 servings

PREP. TIME: 15 minutes

CHILLING TIME: 24 hours

INGREDIENTS:

32-oz can sauerkraut, drained

1 onion, chopped

1 carrot, shredded

2 Tbsp. olive oil

½ red or green sweet pepper, chopped

½ tsp. salt

¾ cup sugar

½ cup cider vinegar

1. Combine all ingredients in bowl with cover.

2. Let stand 24 hours, covered, in refrigerator to blend flavors.

Cider-Glazed Baby Carrots

MAKES: 8 servings

PREP. TIME: 10 minutes

COOKING TIME: 20 minutes

Beginning with fresh or frozen carrots and apple cider, this is ready to serve within half an hour.

INGREDIENTS:

16-oz. bag baby carrots, fresh or frozen (thawed)

1 ½ cups apple cider

1 Tbsp. butter

1 tsp. dried thyme

1 Tbsp. brown sugar

½ tsp. salt

1. In a large skillet over medium-high heat, combine all ingredients and bring to a simmer. Cover and reduce heat; simmer for 10 minutes.

2. Uncover and increase heat to high. Boil, stirring occasionally, until cider has reduced to a thick glaze (5–8 minutes).

3. Remove from stove and serve hot.

Happy Beets

MAKES: 6–8 servings

PREP. TIMIE: 5 minutes

COOKING TIME: 15 minutes

From my first gourmet cooking class at Patchwork Quilt Inn, Middlebury, Indiana in 1975— beets in red wine.

INGREDIENTS:

2 cups pickled beet juice

½ cup dry red wine

2 Tbsp. cornstarch dissolved in ¼ cup water

4 cups small whole pickled beets

1 Tbsp. sugar

½ tsp. salt

1. Heat juice in saucepan over medium heat, stir in wine and dissolved cornstarch. Bring to boil and simmer about 2 minutes, until thickened.

2. Add beets, sugar, and salt and cook until warmed thoroughly.

3. Serve hot.

Carrots Veronique

MAKES: 8 servings

PREP. TIME: 20 minutes

COOKING TIME: 30 minutes total

Also from Patchwork Quilt, this recipe combines cooked carrots and white grapes.

INGREDIENTS:

2 lbs. whole carrots, scraped and cut into ⅓" slices

1 ¼ tsp. salt, divided

½ cup (1 stick) butter

1 cup sugar

⅛ tsp. nutmeg

¼ cup white wine

2 cups seedless green grapes

1. Cook carrots in water to cover with 1 tsp. salt, about 12 minutes. Drain and place in 2-quart baking dish.

2. In small saucepan, melt butter, stirring in sugar, ¼ tsp. salt, and nutmeg until mixture turns light caramel. Add wine and pour over carrots.

3. Bake at 350° for 15 minutes.

4. Add grapes just before serving.

Brussels Sprouts with Cranberry Balsamic

MAKES: 8 servings

PREP. TIME: 20 minutes

COOKING TIME: 8–10 minutes

A more exotic mix of fresh sprouts and dried cranberries, this is another 30-minute dish.

INGREDIENTS:

2 Tbsp. balsamic vinegar

1 Tbsp. water

3 Tbsp. olive oil, *divided*

3 Tbsp. dried cranberries

¼ tsp. salt

2 lbs. Brussels sprouts, stem ends trimmed, outer leaves removed, cut in half

1. To make dressing, combine vinegar, water, 2 Tbsp. oil, cranberries, and salt in a blender or food processor. Pulse until well combined; cranberries should be chopped but not pureed. Add remaining tablespoon of oil as needed.

2. Place the sprouts in a steamer over a saucepan with a few inches of boiling water; steam 5–8 minutes or until fork tender. Alternatively, steam in microwave according to instructions. (If sprouts are a uniform size, they should cook evenly.)

3. Transfer steamed sprouts to serving bowl, add dressing, and toss to coat evenly. Serve warm or at room temperature.

Leeks in Cheese Sauce

MAKES: 4–6 servings

PREP. AND COOKING TIME: 40 minutes

I perfected this recipe in the tiny galley of a narrow boat, cruising on an English country canal.

INGREDIENTS:

6 large leeks

1 ½–2 cups milk

1 bay leaf

3 oz. butter

2 oz. flour

8 oz. strong, hard cheese (such as mature cheddar), grated

¼ tsp. salt

¼ tsp. black pepper

1. Wash leeks well and cut into thick slices. Parboil for 8–10 minutes, drain, and put in 2-quart buttered baking dish.

2. Heat milk in saucepan with bay leaf, then set aside covered for 10 minutes. Remove bay leaf.

3. Melt butter in medium saucepan. Remove from heat and stir in flour, mixing well. Slowly add milk, mixing well and beating. Return pan to heat, stir until sauce boils and thickens. Remove from heat and stir in grated cheese, salt, and pepper. Pour sauce over the leeks.

4. Bake at 400° until golden brown on top, about 10 minutes.

Red Onions with Mushrooms and Fresh Thyme

A winning taste treat ready to serve within 20 minutes.

MAKES: 6 servings

PREP. TIME: 10 minutes

COOKING TIME: 10 minutes

INGREDIENTS:

ONION MIX:

3 Tbsp. olive oil

3 cups red onions, cut in ½" slices (not rings)

½ tsp. coarse salt

¼ tsp. freshly ground black pepper

2 tsp. minced garlic

2 Tbsp. balsamic vinegar

1 tsp. minced fresh thyme leaves

MUSHROOM MIX:

2 Tbsp. olive oil

2 Tbsp. unsalted butter

3 cups shiitake mushroom caps, cut ½" thick

3 cups cremini mushroom caps, cut ½" thick

½ tsp. coarse salt

¼ tsp. coarsely ground pepper

1 tsp. dry thyme leaves, crushed

1. For onions, heat oil in large skillet over medium-high heat. Add onions, salt, and pepper. Cook, stirring often, until slightly browned and just softened, about 10 minutes. Stir in garlic, vinegar, and thyme. Place in serving dish.

2. For mushrooms, in same skillet heat oil and butter over medium-high heat. Add mushrooms, salt, and pepper. Cook, stirring often, until browned but still rather firm, about 4 minutes. Stir in thyme. Add to onions, combine and serve.

Tip: Either mix can be prepared a day ahead and stored in the refrigerator.

Eight decades as host and guest at home and away
1963–1972

The year 1963 provided three food memories. On a Memorial Day family excursion with Joe and Mary Hertzler in Virginia we dined at Chowning's Tavern in historic Williamsburg where my lunch selection was oysters on the half shell from Chesapeake Bay with Chowning's "good bread of unbleached flour, water-ground in the colonial manner." I stole a handwritten French menu in fading ink from Restaurant Raffy in Paris but I no longer remember what I ate. On a short British European Airways flight from Paris to London on July 19, upgraded because I chose to be at the end of the queue, I enjoyed my first and only ever first class air cuisine: Saumon Fume, Supreme de Sole "Viscount," Fromages de France, Peche Conde, and Petits Fours.

On a 1965 family excursion to our nation's capital we visited Evans Farm Inn in McLean, Virginia where our lunch servers were in colonial dress. The fixed menu started with Virginia spiced cider followed by plantation style hickory-smoked young chicken with spoon bread and fresh farm vegetables. I copied this wall hanging quote from Dr. Samuel Johnson: "There is nothing which has yet been contriv'd by Man by which so much Happiness has been produc'd as by a good Tavern or Inn."

My first Atlantic crossing demanded jet-prop refueling stops in Newfoundland and Iceland. For three weeks, as part of an ecumenical youth workers traveling seminar, I was enamored with unfamiliar food and beverage options in Germany, France, and England.

Four years later, as a youth delegate to Mennonite World Conference 1967 in Amsterdam, with add-on excursions, my palate relished new taste combinations. During a circle tour of Denmark, I was endeared to my first authentic Scandinavian specialty buffet at the Kungsholm in Copenhagen where the menu explained that their world famous smorgasbord resulted from more than 500 years of devoted effort. "Some say the custom began in the days of old as a way of celebrating the return of daylight after months of darkness. Doughty Norsemen would gather from miles around, each bringing whatever food he could until tables were laden to overflowing with all manner of fish, meats, cheeses and other delicacies." Patrons were invited to enjoy three separate servings in order: herring and other seafood, hot delicacies, and meats, then tasty salads and cheeses. Certainly a true gourmet ritual!

Then our family was invited to West Africa for five years with Mennonite Board of Missions and I was committed to global cuisine. Returning in 1971 for a second mission term in Ghana, we flew Swissair from Geneva to Accra. Those were the days when economy class menus appeared more like first class and were written in both French and English: Pinot Noir du Valais (Swiss red wine from the upper Rhone Valley); saumon fume with sauce raifort (smoked salmon with horseradish sauce); escalope de veau suzanne/tagliatelli verde (veal scallop/creamed mushrooms and green noodles); pointes d'asperges au beurre (asparagus tips in butter); savarin aux fruits (yeast cake ring with fruit salad); fromage (cheese) and café (coffee).

Along with expatriate friends in Ghana, we used a railroad theme for a traveling food event one February Saturday in 1973. Course by course, the Kumasi (an inland town) Express International Buffet moved from home to home around Ghana's capital city. Food represented places and tastes households had experienced earlier. Petersens prepared egg drop soup and chicken with soy sauce and ginger from Taiwan. Hachtens served kefta and bastilla from Morocco. Belchers joined duro wat from Ethiopia with Adams' pancit from the Philippines. Higbees and Roths brought up the caboose with apple pie and hand-cranked ice cream from the USA topped off with Black Star coffee from our newly adopted homeland.

SWEETS

CAKES

Grandma Roth's Chocolate Cake

MAKES: 12 servings

PREP. TIME: 10 minutes

BAKING TIME: 30 minutes

From paternal grandmother Mary Graber Roth.

INGREDIENTS:

2 eggs

1 cup cream, soured naturally or with 1 Tbs. vinegar

2 tsp. vanilla extract

1 ¼ cups flour

1 cup sugar

¼ cup cocoa powder

¼ tsp. salt

1 tsp. baking soda

1. In bowl, beat eggs; add soured cream and vanilla until well blended.

2. Sift dry ingredients, and add to mixture. Beat well.

3. Pour into greased and floured 8″ x 8″ square pan.

4. Bake in 350° oven for 25 minutes or until toothpick inserted in center comes out clean. Frost with your favorite icing.

Tip: Double recipe for layer cake.

Aunt Barbara's Feather Sponge Cake

MAKES: 16 servings

PREP. TIME: 15 minutes

BAKING TIME: 55 minutes

This recipe, from a maternal great aunt whose Illinois farm kitchen I visited during childhood trips, is almost identical to the recipe for Israel's traditional cake, which has no Hebrew name. Israeli bakers often cut the cake horizontally, covering the bottom layer with berry jelly, fresh strawberries, and whipped cream.

INGREDIENTS:

6 egg yolks

½ cup water

1 ¼ cups sugar

1 Tbs. vanilla extract

1 ½ cups cake flour

¼ tsp. salt

6 egg whites

¾ tsp. cream of tartar

1. In large bowl, beat egg yolks with water until thick, about 5 minutes, then beat in sugar and vanilla before folding in cake flour and salt.

2. In smaller bowl, beat egg whites with cream of tartar until they peak, then fold gently into batter.

3. Pour into ungreased 10″ tube pan, and bake in 325° oven for 55 minutes.

4. Remove from oven, invert to cool; if pan does not have legs invert over bottle.

5. When completely cool, use knife or spatula to loosen edges, and place on serving plate.

Wonder Cake

MAKES: 12 servings

PREP. TIME: 10 minutes

BAKING TIME: 1 hour

Another popular Israeli cake easily prepared to go with late afternoon coffee or tea. It is not considered proper in Israel to offer a hot drink without cake.

INGREDIENTS:

½ cup butter

1 cup sugar

5 egg yolks

2 ¼ cups cake flour

½ tsp. salt

2 tsp. baking powder

¾ cup milk

1 Tbs. vanilla

2 Tbs. confectioner's sugar

1. In bowl, cream butter and sugar with beater. Add one egg yolk at a time, beating after each addition.

2. Sift flour, salt, and baking powder together; add to batter, alternating with milk. Beat in vanilla.

3. Pour batter in greased and floured 9" x 5" loaf pan.

4. Bake in 350° oven for 1 hour or until toothpick in center comes out clean.

5. Cool on a rack; sprinkle with confectioner's sugar.

Rhubarb Cake

MAKES: 16 servings

PREP. TIME: 10 minutes

BAKING TIME: 30 minutes

Niece Patty's recipe, found with Mother Roth's favorites.

INGREDIENTS:

1 ¼ cups brown sugar

1 egg

½ cup butter, melted (one stick)

2 Tbs. olive oil

¼ cup peach or apple butter

1 cup milk

1 Tbs. white vinegar

¾ tsp. salt

1 tsp. baking soda

1 cup flour

1 cup whole-wheat flour

1 ½ cups fresh or frozen rhubarb, finely chopped

½ cup walnuts, chopped

2 tsp. vanilla extract

1. In large bowl, blend brown sugar, egg, butter, olive oil, and peach butter.

2. In another bowl, combine milk, white vinegar, salt, and soda.

3. Alternate milk mixture and flours as you add them to sugar and egg mixture.

4. Stir rhubarb, walnuts, and vanilla into batter.

5. Pour into greased and floured 9" x 13" baking pan.

6. Bake in 350° oven for 30 minutes or until toothpick comes out clean.

7. Serve warm or cold with whipped cream topped with cinnamon.

Mom's Favorite Chocolate Cake

MAKES: 16 servings

PREP. TIME: 10 minutes

BAKING TIME: 30 minutes

From Mother Minnie Wenger Roth.

INGREDIENTS:

2 cups flour

2 cups sugar

½ cup cocoa powder

2 tsp. baking soda

1 tsp. baking powder

½ tsp. salt

2 eggs

½ cup oil

1 cup hot coffee

1 cup milk

1 Tbs. vanilla extract

¼ cup confectioner's sugar

1. In bowl, sift first six ingredients.

2. In another bowl, beat eggs with oil; then slowly add coffee, milk, and vanilla.

3. In larger third bowl, stir dry and liquid ingredients together, alternating between the mixtures.

4. Pour in greased and floured 9" x 13" baking pan.

5. Bake in 350° oven for 30 minutes or until toothpick in center comes out clean.

6. Cool and dust with confectioner's sugar.

Marshmallow Cake

MAKES: 16 servings

PREP. TIME: 10 minutes

RESTING TIME: 12 hours or overnight

BAKING TIME: 35 minutes

A unique white cake from Mother Roth, but marshmallows are not an ingredient.

INGREDIENTS:

2 cups cake flour

2 cups sugar

1 cup boiling water

2 tsp. baking powder

6 egg whites

½ tsp. cream of tartar

1. In bowl with cover, sift together flour and sugar; stir in boiling water until blended.

2. Cover, and leave overnight at room temperature.

3. Add baking powder to batter.

4. In smaller bowl, beat egg whites until firm, adding cream of tartar. Fold gently into batter.

5. Spoon into ungreased, floured 9″ x 13″ pan.

6. Have oven preheated to 375°; turn back to 350° when inserting cake and leave at this temperature for the 35 minute baking time or until toothpick inserted in center comes out clean. Cool.

Pioneer Economy Cake

MAKES: 16 servings

PREP. TIME: 20 minutes

RESTING TIME: 30 minutes

BAKING TIME: 50 minutes

From a 1910 cookbook from Dr. Miles Medical Co., Elkhart, Indiana.

INGREDIENTS:

1 cup water

1 cup brown sugar

1 cup raisins

⅜ cup lard (I use butter)

1 tsp. ground nutmeg

1 tsp. ground cinnamon

½ tsp. salt

2 ¼ cups flour

2 tsp. baking powder

1 tsp. baking soda

½ cup nuts, chopped "will add to the flavor"

1. In saucepan over medium heat, bring first seven ingredients to boiling; boil for 2 minutes. Remove from stove, and let stand until cool (about 30 minutes).

2. Sift flour, baking powder, and baking soda together, and add to cooked mixture, stirring until blended. Add nuts. Pour into 9" x 13" greased, floured pan.

3. Bake in 350° oven about 50 minutes or until toothpick inserted in center comes out clean.

4. Cool, and serve with or without frosting of choice.

Stevenson Farm's Apple Cake

MAKES: 16 servings

PREP. TIME: 10 minutes

BAKING TIME: 45 minutes

From a family farm restaurant on Route 40 near Kansas City, opened in 1946— once discovered, it has been a Roth required stop on any road trip crossing Missouri.

INGREDIENTS:

¼ cup butter

1 cup sugar

1 egg

4 cups apples, chopped

1 cup flour

1 tsp. baking soda

⅛ tsp. salt

2 tsp. ground cinnamon

½ tsp. ground nutmeg

¼ tsp. ground cloves

1. In bowl, cream butter and sugar. Mix in egg and apples.

2. In another bowl, sift together remaining ingredients and add to apple mixture, mixing well (batter is thick).

3. Spread in greased 9″ x 9″ baking pan.

4. Bake in 325° oven about 45 minutes or until toothpick inserted in center comes out clean. Remove from oven.

5. While warm, cut into equal squares. Sprinkle with confectioner's sugar.

Guinness Chocolate Layer Cake

MAKES: 16 servings

ICING PREP. TIME: 20 minutes

CAKE AND SYRUP PREP. TIME: 45 minutes

RESTING TIME: 24 hours

BAKING TIME: 30 minutes

A labor intensive Celtic desert from the legendary Irish pub Kells in Portland, Oregon.

INGREDIENTS:

BITTERSWEET ICING

1 ½ cups heavy cream

6 oz. bittersweet chocolate, finely chopped

5 Tbs. confectioner's sugar

4 Tbs. cocoa powder (¼ cup)

2 tsp. vanilla extract

⅛ tsp. salt

For the icing:

1. In pan, bring cream to a boil.

2. Put chocolate in heatproof bowl (will need a cover), pour cream over it, whisking until melted and combined. Cover tightly, and chill a day ahead.

3. Up to 3 hours before serving cake, whip chilled chocolate with electric hand beater, using chilled beaters. When soft peaks form, sift in confectioner's sugar and cocoa, add vanilla and salt, and continue whipping until combined.

DRIZZLING SYRUP

⅓ cup Draft Guinness Stout (measure after foam subsides)

3 Tbs. cocoa powder

2 tsp. vanilla extract

For the syrup:

1. In small heavy pan, combine all ingredients, whisking until smooth.

2. Heat over medium heat until sugar dissolves and syrup is smooth.

CAKE

⅔ cup Draft Guinness Stout (measure after foam subsides)

⅔ cup currants

½ cup + 2 Tbs. cocoa powder

¼ cup semi-sweet chocolate chips

¾ cup buttermilk

⅔ cup unsalted butter, softened

1 ½ cups + 2 Tbs. sugar

4 eggs

2 tsp. vanilla

2 cups + 2 Tbs. flour

1 ½ tsp. baking soda

½ tsp. baking powder

¼ tsp. salt

½ cup red currant jelly, warmed

1 cup walnut halves

For the cake:

1. In bowl (will need cover), pour stout over currants, and soak 30 minutes; drain, reserving stout in small pan. Over medium heat, whisk in ½ cup cocoa, and bring to simmer; remove from heat, add chocolate chips, stirring until melted. Cool slightly; then stir in buttermilk.

2. In separate bowl, beat butter at medium speed until smooth, gradually adding sugar until blended. Beat in eggs, one at a time. Beat in vanilla.

3. Combine flour, baking soda, baking powder, and salt. Alternate between flour mixture and chocolate mixture as you add them to butter mixture, stirring until blended (may look curdled). Stir in currants.

4. Combine the remaining 2 Tbs. of each: cocoa, sugar, and flour. Grease two 9″ round cake pans, and dust with cocoa mixture.

5. Divide batter between pans. Bake in 350° oven for 25 minutes or until toothpick inserted in center comes out clean. Cool in pans on wire rack 10 minutes; then invert pans on rack.

6. Poke tops of layers with skewer or toothpick. Drizzle syrup over tops. Place one layer on a platter; spread warmed jelly over it. Chill 30 minutes. Then, cover jelly with about one-fourth of the bittersweet icing. Place second layer on top.

7. Ice top and sides of cake with remaining icing. Press nuts into sides of cake.

CANDIES
AND COOKIES

Quick and Easy Energy Bars

Inspired by a recipe from Verena Eicher, teenage daughter of Amish Cook columnist Lavina Eicher, these bars satisfy both my genetic sweet tooth and my intentions to eat healthily.

MAKES: 16 2" x 3" bars

PREP. TIME: 10 minutes

BAKING TIME: 20 minutes

INGREDIENTS:

2 cups quick cooking oats

2 cups crispy rice cereal

½ cup honey

½ cup brown sugar

½ cup chunky peanut butter

½ cup toasted sunflower seeds

½ cup dark chocolate chips

1. Mix all ingredients in bowl, and press into a greased 9" x 13" pan.

2. In 350° oven, bake 18–20 minutes.

3. Cool; cut into 16 equal-sized bars.

Vincent's Peanut Butter Fudge

MAKES: 20 pieces

PREP. TIME: 10 minutes

COOKING TIME: 10 minutes

Vincent Krabill was my teacher when I entered Stringtown Elementary School in Noble, Iowa, when I entered Wayland High School (Iowa), and when I entered Hesston College (Kansas). My hunch is that few students can claim the same teacher for these three academic portals. A teacher at Hesston for 25 years, Vincent developed this recipe to welcome students to his home adjoining the campus. My recipe is adapted from Hesston College Centennial Cookbook, *page 512.*

INGREDIENTS:

½ cup canola or olive oil

1 cup sugar

1 cup brown sugar

¾ cup powdered baking cocoa

½ cup 1% milk

⅛ tsp. salt

½ cup crunchy peanut butter

1 Tbsp. vanilla

3 cups dry quick oatmeal

½ cup coconut (optional)

1. In microwave-safe bowl, blend first six ingredients. Heat in microwave on high until boiling (about 6 minutes).

2. Stir in remaining ingredients, and pour into well-greased 10″ square pan.

3. Cool, and cut into squares.

Rice Marshmallow Squares

MAKES: 35 2"x 2" squares

PREP. TIME: 15 minutes

COOLING TIME: 10 minutes

My guests, children of all ages, never tire of this quick and healthy treat.

INGREDIENTS:

½ cup butter (1 stick)

½ cup margarine (1 stick)

16-oz. package miniature marshmallows (2 cups)

2 Tbs. vanilla extract

13 ½-oz. package crispy rice cereal

1. In Dutch oven over medium heat, melt butter and margarine. Add marshmallows, stirring constantly until blended.

2. Remove from stove, add vanilla. Gradually pour cereal into this mixture, stirring well as you do so.

3. Transfer to 10" x 14" greased baking sheet, pressing down to fill pan evenly. Cut into squares.

Tip: Use wax paper over rice-marshmallow mixture; press firmly with fingers to level it out.

Tip: Mix in 4-oz. miniature candy dots before transferring to baking sheet.

Bourbon Balls

MAKES: about 40 ¾" balls

PREP. TIME: 10 minutes

This traditional holiday confection pleases my guests any time of year.

INGREDIENTS:

2 cups graham crackers, finely crushed

1 cup confectioner's sugar, plus ¼ cup for dusting

¼ cup dark cocoa powder

1 cup pecans, finely chopped

1 ½ Tbs. honey

¼ cup rum

1. Mix dry ingredients until combined.

2. Stir in honey and rum, blending with hands (buttered fingers) until mixture is moldable.

3. Form into balls about ¾" in diameter. Roll in sugar. Eat, serve, or store.

Tip: Flavor enhances when aged in tightly covered tin for a week or more.

Chocolate Cherry Clusters

MAKES: about 36 pieces

PREP. TIME: 10 minutes

COOLING TIME: 2 hours

INGREDIENTS:

2 cups bittersweet
   chocolate chips

1 ½ cups oat circle cereal

1 cup dried sweet cherries

½ cup walnut pieces

1. In medium bowl, microwave chocolate chips on high 1 minute. Stir. Microwave 1 minute more. Stir until smooth.

2. Remove from microwave; quickly stir in remaining ingredients until well coated.

3. Using a tablespoon, drop clusters on baking sheet.

4. Refrigerate at least 2 hours until no longer sticky.

Anise Can't-Eat-Just-One Cookies

Licorice is one of my favorite flavors, whether in long sticks, black jelly beans, peppernut cookies, or these aptly labeled "can't-eat-just-one" cookies.

MAKES: about 48 cookies

PREP.TIME: 15 minutes

CHILLING TIME: 3 hours (or overnight)

BAKING TIME: 30 minutes

INGREDIENTS:

½ cup unsalted butter

½ cup olive oil

½ cup sugar

½ cup brown sugar

1 egg

1 Tbs. vanilla extract

1 tsp. anise flavoring

1 cup flour

1 cup whole wheat flour

½ tsp. salt

½ tsp. baking powder

½ cup old-fashioned rolled oats

1. In bowl, cream butter and olive oil, stirring in sugars gradually. Add egg, vanilla, and anise.
2. In separate bowl, mix together flours, salt, and baking powder.
3. Alternate between flour mixture and rolled oats as you add them to butter mixture for a stiff dough.
4. Form into three rolls. Wrap in plastic or waxed paper, and chill at least 3 hours or overnight.
5. When ready to bake, slice into cookies of ¼" thickness. Bake in 400° oven on greased cookie sheets for about 10 minutes. Cool on rack.

Preacher Cookies

MAKES: 36 cookies or 32 1" x 2" bars

PREP. TIME: 10 minutes

A pastor's spouse from the Bible Belt gave me this no-bake recipe, passed along from generation to generation. She used it often when confronted with the need for a short-notice sweet to serve with hot drinks to drop-in guests.

INGREDIENTS:

1 cup sugar

½ cup butter (1 stick)

½ cup milk

2 cups quick oatmeal

½ cup cocoa powder

½ tsp. salt

2 tsp. vanilla extract

1. In pan, combine sugar, butter, and milk. Over medium heat, bring to full boil; then cook 3 minutes longer, stirring constantly.

2. Continue stirring, adding oatmeal, cocoa, salt, and vanilla. Remove from stove.

3. Spoon warm dough by heaping teaspoons on waxed paper, or spread in 8" pan for bars; cool before serving.

Tip: Shredded coconut or chopped nuts may be substituted for cocoa.

Tip: Refrigeration quickens cooling.

Best-Ever Sugar Cookies

MAKES: 30 to 36 cookies

PREP. TIME: 15 minutes

BAKING TIME: 10–12 minutes per sheet of 12

My brother Larry does not swear. But if he did, he maintains this recipe results in melt-in-your mouth white sugar cookies which cannot be beat. Since he's my brother (albeit younger), I take his word seriously.

INGREDIENTS:

1 cup confectioner's sugar

1 cup sugar, plus sugar to sprinkle

1 cup (2 sticks) butter

1 cup canola oil

2 eggs

1 tsp. vanilla extract

1 tsp. baking soda

½ tsp. salt

2 tsp. cream of tartar

4 ½ cups flour

1. In bowl, cream sugars, butter, and canola oil. Add eggs and vanilla.

2. In a separate bowl, mix soda, salt, and cream of tartar with flour. Add flour mixture to creamed butter mixture; stir until well mixed.

3. Drop by rounded tablespoons onto cookie sheet. Flatten with a glass dipped in sugar. Sprinkle sugar on top of cookies. In 350° oven, bake each sheet 10–12 minutes.

4. Cool on rack before enjoying or storing.

Denver Chocolate Chip Oatmeal Cookies

MAKES: 24 to 30 cookies, depending on size

PREP. TIME: 15 minutes

BAKING TIME: 10 minutes per sheet of 8–10

My granddaughters agree with the editors of 5280 magazine: here ends the search for the perfect chocolate-chip treat. Using M&Ms packages as cushioning, the cookies are easily packed and protected for collegiate care packages, for any occasion—or no occasion at all.

INGREDIENTS:

1 cup unsalted butter (2 sticks), softened but not melted

1 cup brown sugar

¾ cup sugar

1 tsp. salt

1 tsp. baking soda

2 eggs

1 tsp. vanilla extract

2 cups flour (up to 1 cup can be whole wheat pastry flour)

2 cups old fashioned oats (not instant)

2 cups mini chocolate chips

2 cups pecans, chopped but not toasted

1. Cream together butter and sugars for about 5 minutes (paddle attachment on a stand mixer works well). Add salt and baking soda.

2. Using electric mixer on low speed, add the eggs, one at a time, until incorporated. Do not overmix. Add vanilla. Mix in flour at low speed until incorporated. Add oats, chocolate chips, and chopped pecans, only until combined. (Overmixing results in tough cookies.)

3. Drop heaping tablespoons of dough onto parchment-lined baking sheet. In 375° oven, bake about 8–10 minutes or until golden brown.

4. Cool briefly on baking sheet before transferring to wire rack.

PIES AND PUDDINGS

Cape Cod Baked Indian Pudding

MAKES: 8 servings

PREP. TIME: 30 minutes

BAKING TIME: 2 ½ hours

Water-powered gristmills fascinate me, which may explain why my kitchen bias leans toward stone ground grains. My local Elkhart County source for such is the early 19th century Bonneyville Mill, the oldest continuously operated gristmill in Indiana. Several summers ago, while exploring Cape Cod, I was pleased to discover Dexter Grist Mill in Sandwich, MA. Dating back two centuries earlier to 1654, Dexter's wooden water wheel and simple gear design represent the earliest milling machinery in America. Three bags of stone ground cornmeal entitled us to a collection of recipes including this Native American dish which I sampled at the neighboring Plymouth Plantation.

INGREDIENTS:

3 cups + 1 cup whole milk

⅓ cup sorghum molasses

4 Tbs. stone ground cornmeal

½ cup brown sugar

1 egg, beaten

1 Tbs. butter

¼ tsp. salt

½ tsp. ginger

1 tsp. cinnamon

1. Scald 3 cups milk in saucepan; stir in molasses and cornmeal, and cook until thickened, stirring constantly to prevent scorching.

2. Remove from heat, add remaining ingredients (except the last cup of milk), and mix thoroughly.

3. Pour into 8" x 8" well-buttered glass baking dish, and bake 30 minutes in 350° oven.

4. Pour remaining 1 cup milk over pudding, and continue baking for 120 minutes longer.

5. Serve warm or cold with whipped cream or ice cream.

Pumpkin Almost-Pie

MAKES: 8 servings

PREP. TIME: 15 minutes

BAKING TIME: 60 minutes

INGREDIENTS:

½ cup sugar

½ cup baking mix

2 eggs, beaten

15-oz. can pumpkin puree

1 Tbs. butter, melted

¼ cup applesauce

1 15-oz. can non-fat
   evaporated milk

1 Tbs. pumpkin pie spice

1 Tbs. vanilla extract

1. In bowl, mix all ingredients in order, and pour into greased 9″ pie pan.

2. In 350° oven, bake for 1 hour.

French Chocolate Custard (pots de crème au chocolat)

MAKES: 6 servings

PREP. TIME: 15 minutes

BAKING TIME: 30 minutes

INGREDIENTS:

1 ½ cups half-and-half

6-oz. pkg. semisweet chocolate chips

3 eggs

⅓ cup + 1 Tbs. sugar

⅛ tsp. salt

½ cup whipping cream

2 Tbs. brandy or crème de menthe

1. In saucepan over medium heat, stir half-and-half with chocolate chips until smooth. Cool slightly.

2. In bowl, beat eggs with ⅛ cup sugar and salt. Gradually stir into chocolate mixture.

3. Divide into 6 ungreased 6-oz ovenproof cups.

4. Place cups in baking dish on oven rack. Pour boiling water into pan within ½" of tops of cups.

5. Bake in 350° oven for 25 minutes. Remove cups from water; cool slightly.

6. Cover with plastic wrap, and refrigerate at least 4 hours but no longer than 24.

7. Before serving, whip cream in chilled bowl, add remaining 1 Tbs. sugar, and fold in liquor. Divide among the 6 cups.

Aunt Effie's Rhubarb Pudding

MAKES: 10 servings

PREP TIME: 10 minutes

BAKING TIME: 30 minutes

Great Uncle Joe and Aunt Effie Good never had grandchildren of their own, so they spoiled their nephews and nieces. Most years their farm rhubarb patch provided an abundant source for Aunt Effie's pudding. Her recipe found its way into my mother's collection, which I inherited.

INGREDIENTS:

2 cups rhubarb, chopped (fresh or frozen)

1 cup sugar, *divided*

1 Tbs. butter

1 egg

¾ cup half and half

½ cup flour

½ cup whole wheat flour

1 tsp. baking powder

1. In greased baking casserole, mix rhubarb, ½ cup sugar, and butter.

2. In separate bowl, whisk egg, half and half, and remaining ½ cup sugar. Mix in both flours and baking powder. Pour over rhubarb.

3. In 375° oven, bake for 30 minutes. Serve warm or room temperature with whipped cream or ice cream.

Double Apricot Pie

MAKES: 8 servings

PREP. TIME: 10 minutes (using prepared pie crust)

BAKING TIME: 25 minutes

INGREDIENTS:

Prepared pie crust (bottom shell and top)

20 large dried apricots

¼ cup water

½ cup sugar

2 Tbs. cornstarch

1 tsp. minute tapioca

2 Tbs. apricot brandy

15-oz. can apricots in heavy syrup

1 Tbs. sugar

1. In saucepan over medium heat, cook dried apricots in water until tender.

2. In bowl, mix sugar, cornstarch, tapioca, and brandy until smooth. Stir in the cooked, dried apricots and canned apricots with heavy syrup.

3. Spoon into unbaked pie shell, cover with top crust, and sprinkle with sugar.

4. In 400° oven, bake for 10 minutes. Reduce heat to 350°, and bake for 20 more minutes or until crust is nicely browned.

Tip: Refrigerated (not frozen) Pillsbury crusts are the choice in my kitchen.

Frozen Grand Marnier Mousse

MAKES: 12 servings

PREP. TIME: 1 hour

RESTING TIME: 24 hours minimum

A missionary friend working in France discovered this spectacular centerpiece for a dessert buffet. It is worth all the time invested and can be prepared up to a week before serving.

INGREDIENTS:

⅓ cup + ¼ cup sugar

1 envelope unflavored gelatin

2 tsp. cornstarch

6 egg yolks

1 cup milk

⅓ cup Grand Marnier

4 egg whites

2 cups heavy whipping cream, divided

1 pint fresh strawberries, washed and halved

2 kiwis, pared and sliced

1. In medium saucepan, combine ⅓ cup sugar, gelatin, and cornstarch; add egg yolks, and beat until blended. Gradually stir in milk. Over medium heat, cook, stirring constantly just until slightly thickened. Remove from heat, and stir in liqueur.

2. Set pan in larger pan filled with crushed ice and water. Chill, stirring often, until mixture mounds when spooned.

3. While mixture is chilling, in medium bowl, beat egg whites with electric beater until double in volume. Beat in remaining ¼ cup sugar gradually until meringue forms soft peaks.

4. In small chilled bowl, beat 1 ½ cups of heavy whipping cream until stiff.

5. Fold whipped cream into gelatin mixture; then fold in meringue until no streaks of white remain.

6. Pour into 8-cup ring mold, and smooth the top. Cover with plastic wrap. Freeze overnight or up to one week.

7. To serve, remove mousse from freezer. Loosen around edges with spatula. Unmold onto serving platter. Beat remaining ½ cup cream until stiff. Pipe whipped cream around base and top of mousse. Garnish with berries and kiwi slices.

Karen's Graham Cracker Fluff

MAKES: 12 servings

PREP. TIME: 25 minutes

CHILLING TIME: at least 3 hours

INGREDIENTS:

1 envelope unflavored gelatin

½ cup water (room temperature)

2 egg yolks

⅓ cup + 3 Tbs. sugar

⅔ cup milk

1 cup whipping cream

1 Tbs. vanilla extract

2 egg whites

3 Tbs. butter, melted

18 graham crackers, crushed

1. In bowl, soak gelatin in water.

2. In cooking pan, beat egg yolks with ⊠ cup sugar. Over medium heat, gradually stir in milk, and cook until it begins to thicken. Pour hot mixture over gelatin, and stir until smooth. Chill until slightly thickened.

3. In separate chilled bowl, whip cream until it peaks; stir in vanilla.

4. With clean beaters, in another bowl, beat egg whites until stiff. Alternately, fold whipped cream and egg whites into chilled cooked gelatin mixture.

5. In 9" x 14" glass pan, combine butter, crushed graham crackers, and remaining 3 Tbs. sugar. Press into bottom, reserving about ⅓ for topping. Pour pudding over graham cracker bottom; smooth, and top with reserved crumbs. Chill at least 3 hours before serving.

Tip: I like to add a 6-oz can of crushed pineapple to the fluff just before putting in pan to chill.

Chocolate Graham Pumpkin Trifle

MAKES: 10 servings

PREP. TIME: 45 minutes

INGREDIENTS:

8 oz. (1 cup) chocolate graham crackers

¼ cup candied ginger (also called crystallized)

16-oz. pound cake

4 ½ cups heavy cream, divided

1 ¼ cup confectioner's sugar, divided

2 Tbs. vanilla extract, divided

16-oz. can pumpkin puree

1 tsp. pumpkin pie spice

1. In food processor, combine graham crackers and ginger; process until they are fine crumbs.

2. Cut pound cake into 1″ cubes. Arrange half the cubes on bottom of glass trifle dish.

3. In large chilled bowl, beat 2 cups of heavy cream to form stiff peaks; fold in ¼ cup confectioner's sugar and 1 Tbs. vanilla. Spoon two-thirds of the whipped cream over cake cubes, smoothing into a single layer. Sprinkle the graham cracker-ginger crumb mixture over the cream in an even layer.

4. To the remaining whipped cream, add the canned pumpkin, ½ cup confectioner's sugar, pumpkin pie spice, and ½ cup heavy cream. Beat with electric mixer until thick. Spoon over crumb layer, then smooth evenly.

5. Arrange remaining cake cubes over pumpkin pie layer. At this point, trifle can be refrigerated for up to six hours.

6. Just before serving, in clean chilled bowl with clean mixer beaters, beat remaining 2 cups of heavy cream with remaining ½ cup confectioner's sugar until cream peaks; then add remaining 1 Tbs. vanilla. Spoon over cake layer. Decorate top with candy corn or candy pumpkins.

Janice's Caramel Apple Tart

MAKES: 8 servings

PREP. TIME: 30 minutes

BAKING TIME: 70 minutes

Sister Janice's autumn delicacy is a great substitute for caramel apples and much easier on aging teeth.

INGREDIENTS:

CRUST

¾ cups flour

¾ cups whole wheat flour

1 Tbs. sugar

⅓ cup Parmesan cheese, grated

¼ tsp. crushed red pepper

¼ tsp. salt.

½ cup (1 stick) butter (cold)

3 Tbs. ice water

3 Tbs. breadcrumbs, finely crushed

FILLING

5 Granny Smith apples, cored and sliced

1 cup sugar

3 Tbs. flour

1 Tbs. cinnamon

TOPPING

¾ cup brown sugar

½ cup whole wheat flour

¼ cup butter, cold

2 tsp. vanilla

1. In bowl, mix first six ingredients with electric beater. Cut in butter until mixture resembles coarse crumbs; add water. (Do not over mix; mixture will hold together when pressed between your fingers).

2. Press mixture into bottom and up sides of well-greased 9" springform pan. Sprinkle bread crumbs over the crust.

3. In bowl, gently combine filling ingredients, and pour into crust.

4. In same bowl used for filling, combine topping ingredients, cut together, and sprinkle over filling in tart crust.

5. In 350° oven, bake for 60 minutes, or until top is golden brown. Remove from oven.

6. Divide in 8 equal portions, and drizzle with warm butterscotch caramel sauce of cook's choice before serving.

Tip: My choice butterscotch caramel sauce is made as follows. Mix in saucepan: ¾ cup sugar, ½ cup light corn syrup, ¼ tsp salt, ¼ cup butter, and ½ cup whipping cream. Cook over low heat, stirring to 234° (soft ball). Stir in another ½ cup cream; cook to smooth consistency at 228°. Remove from heat, stir in 1 tsp. vanilla extract. (Makes 2 cups) My sister says: "True caramel flavor, super-smooth, easy to make and keeps in refrigerator."

FRUIT AND FROZEN DESSERTS

Quick-n-Easy Lite Fruit Cobbler

MAKES: 6 servings

PREP. TIME: 10 minutes

RESTING TIME: 20 minutes

BAKING TIME: 45 minutes

INGREDIENTS:

3 cups peaches or berries, fresh or frozen

1 cup sugar, divided

½ cup butter (1 stick)

¼ cup baby food prune sauce

½ cup all-purpose flour

½ cup whole wheat flour

1 tsp. baking powder

1 cup milk

TOPPING

¼ cup brown sugar

1 Tbs. cinnamon

1. In bowl, combine fruit and ½ cup sugar; let stand at room temperature 20 minutes.
2. Melt butter in 1 ½ qt baking dish; mix with prune sauce.
3. In another bowl, sift remaining dry ingredients together, and combine with milk—lumps will remain.
4. Pour into baking dish, mixing lightly with prune-butter sauce. Top batter with fruit.
5. Bake at 350° for 45 minutes. Remove, and sprinkle with topping.
6. Serve warm or room temperature with frozen dessert of choice.

Alice's Cherry Angel Dessert

MAKES: 8 servings

PREP. TIME: 10 minutes

CHILLING TIME: 1 hour

INGREDIENTS:

4-oz. pkg. instant vanilla pudding

1 cup sour cream

1 ½ cups milk.

1 tsp. vanilla extract

16-oz. loaf angel food cake, cut in ½" cubes

15-oz. can cherry pie filling

1. In chilled bowl with electric mixer, beat pudding, sour cream, and milk until thick. Add vanilla extract.

2. Fold in cake cubes.

3. Pour into 8" x 10" cake pan. Cover with pie filling. Chill at least 1 hour before serving.

Tip: Other fruit fillings of choice can be used.

Pears Poached in Red Wine

MAKES: 6 servings

PREP. TIME: 10 minutes

COOKING TIME: 40 minutes

INGREDIENTS:

6 whole pears, peeled and cored but stem left intact

750 ml. bottle red wine of cook's choice

2 cinnamon sticks, halved

4 whole cloves

¾ cup sugar

¼ cup walnuts, toasted and chopped

Crème fraiche for garnish

1. With melon baller, working from bottom up, scoop out pear cores to create a hollow inside resembling a bell.

2. In saucepan of exact size to fit the 6 pears, standing upright, combine wine, spices and sugar. Stand pears upright. Over medium heat bring to simmer, then simmer until pears are almost tender, about 40 minutes. Turn fruit occasionally to poach evenly.

3. In 6 individual dessert dishes divide walnuts. Arrange pears with stem up on walnut bed, sprinkle with blue cheese, top with dollop of crème fraiche.

Crème fraiche
In bowl with cover stir together ½ cup buttermilk and 1 cup whipping cream. Let stand at room temperature for 24 hours; stir and place in clean container. Cover and refrigerate up to a week.

Tip: Remaining spiced wine sauce may be used in salad dressing or as dessert topping.

Tip: Halve pears and poach with blackberries and varied spices.

Peach Syllabub

MAKES: 4 servings

PREP. TIME: 15 minutes

INGREDIENTS:

1 cup whipping cream, well chilled

½ cup confectioner's sugar, *divided*

1 tsp. vanilla extract

2 egg whites

1 Tbs. peach schnapps

2 Tbs. cream sherry

2 cups peaches (fresh or frozen), sliced

1. In chilled bowl, beat cream until it peaks. Fold in ¼ cup sugar; add vanilla.

2. In another bowl, with clean beaters, beat egg whites until stiff; then gently add remaining ¼ cup sugar.

3. Gently blend cream mixture into egg whites; add peach schnapps and sherry.

4. Distribute peaches among 4 dessert dishes, about ½ cup in each. Divide whipped mixture over fruit.

5. Serve immediately or refrigerate for up to an hour.

Peach Granita

MAKES: 4 servings

PREP. TIME: 10 minutes

COOKING TIME: 30 minutes

COOLING TIME: 1 hour

FREEZING TIME: 1 hour

Granita, an Italian word for fruit ice, was probably first made in Sicily.

INGREDIENTS:

1 ½ cups water, boiling

1 lb. fresh peaches, washed and sliced but unpeeled

¼ cup sugar

2 Tbsp. fresh lemon juice

2 Tbsp. peach schnapps

1 tsp. vanilla extract

1. In pan add peaches and sugar to boiling water. Simmer 30 minutes. Cool 1 hour.

2. In blender combine cooled peaches with lemon juice, schnapps, and vanilla for 1 minute.

3. Pour into glass pan or bowl and freeze for 1 hour, scraping every 15 minutes.

4. Spoon into chilled white wine glasses. Serve immediately.

Cherries Jubilee

MAKES: 8 servings

PREP. TIME: 10 minutes

COOKING TIME: 10 minutes

INGREDIENTS:

19-oz. can pitted cherries of cook's choice, juice reserved

¼ cup sugar

1 Tbsp. cornstarch

⅓ cup cherry brandy

1. In bowl whisk sugar, cornstarch, and reserved juice.

2. In skillet over medium heat cook until thick, stirring constantly; add drained cherries.

3. In microwave, warm brandy 30 seconds; pour over cherries and flame at table!

4. Spoon warm cherries over ice cream previously dipped in glass dishes.

Ice Cream Sundaes Times Two

EACH RECIPE MAKES: 1 serving

PREP. TIME: 5 minutes each

INGREDIENTS:

PEACH RHUMBA

½ peach, cooked

1 tsp. rum

1 scoop vanilla ice cream

1 tsp. peach schnapps

1 Tbsp. whipped cream

1 Tbsp. toasted almonds, chopped

1 cherry with stem

1. Into glass stem sundae dish, place peach half hollow side up. Pour rum into hollow.

2. Top with ice cream. Pour schnapps over top. Garnish with whipped cream, nuts, and cherry.

FLAMING SUNDAE

1 scoop each: vanilla, chocolate, strawberry ice cream

1 Tbsp each: chocolate, pineapple, strawberry syrup

3 Tbsp. whipped cream

½ banana

3 cherries with stems

sugar cube

1 Tbsp. lemon extract

1. In bottom of bowl, arrange ice cream. Top each: chocolate over vanilla, pineapple over chocolate, strawberry over strawberry. Fill cracks with whipped cream.

2. Place banana in middle as candle with a cherry on each ice cream mound.

3. Soak sugar cube in extract, place on banana, and light with match just before serving.

Sweet Summer Surprise

MAKES: 6 servings

PREP. TIME: 15 minutes

CHILLING TIME: at least 4 hours

INGREDIENTS:

1 cup seedless grapes, halved

1 cup fresh strawberries, halved

1 cup fresh peaches, sliced bite-sized

1 cup fresh blueberries

¾ cup light brown sugar

1 cup sour cream

1 cup Greek vanilla yogurt

1. In 9″ x 12″ glass dish, combine fruit and mix well. Sprinkle brown sugar over fruit. Top with sour cream and yogurt mixed together. Cover with plastic wrap.

2. Refrigerate at least 4 hours. Before serving, gently stir fruit and spoon into sherbet glasses.

Tip: Other fresh fruits may be used instead of strawberries (for example, kiwi, plums, raspberries) but not bananas; peaches, grapes, and blueberries, however, are essential.

Rothwood Hand-Cranked Ice Cream

This is the foundational family recipe coming from both my maternal Wenger and paternal Roth sides of the ancestral tree. Childhood memories surround the White Mountain hand-cranked freezer, continuously turned until our youthful muscles could turn no longer and Dad took over.
The freezer patent is three years older (1843) than the state of my birth.

MAKES: 12 servings

PREP. TIME: 15 minutes

FREEZING TIME: 20 minutes

INGREDIENTS:

6 eggs

1 ½ cups sugar

2 3-oz pkg. vanilla instant pudding mix

8-oz can sweetened condensed milk

1 pt. whipping cream

2 tsp. vanilla extract (Watkins preferred)

About 3 qts. milk

1. In electric mixer bowl, beat eggs before blending sugar and pudding mix. Beat in condensed milk and whipping cream. Add vanilla.

2. Pour in chilled ice cream freezer, then add milk until container is ⅔ full.

Tip: For variety use chocolate pudding and chocolate milk for chocolate flavor, or butterscotch pudding and pecans for butter pecan.

Freezing tips: Mix and chill at least 24 hours for a smoother, creamier product. Use plenty of salt to ensure brine around the can (if it takes more than 22–25 minutes, you have not used enough salt. Remove dasher and consider it a perk for the ice cream maker. Drain about ½ of the brine, add fresh ice and salt—will hold for 6 to 8 hours.

Eight decades as host and guest at home and away
1973–1982

Often a cookbook or a souvenir menu marked a new food memory, frequently cross-cultural. On a real rail journey across Canada with both Roth and Metzler parents, we hosted a 1978 Mother's Day lunch at Chateau Lake Louise, a Canadian Pacific hotel in Alberta. The menu featured pan-fried fillet of Atlantic sole with brown butter sauce and capers topped off with bread and butter custard pudding.

Walking, or as the English say, rambling, has often combined two of my favorite pastimes: healthy exercise and healthy eating. While on sabbatical in England's West Midlands I journaled one experience dated 6 March 1982. In spite of threatening rain and discernible drizzle we set off from Selly Oak with a West Midlands Family Day Ticket on the cross city express coach for Shenstone. Individual filter coffees at the Plough and Harrow warmed intestines and hearts with courage to weather the elements. The publican assured us the footpath to Wall would be solid underfoot in spite of the rain—he was right, from time to time. Terrain varied: an overgrown, almost untrimmed hedge path we barely squeezed through, over a style to the pasture where a half dozen horses grazed, across a clever concrete foot bridge engineered so that humans but not animals might pass; a drilled field of grain just greening, over a rail bridge, into a not too cleanly harvested turnip field and much stony soil, then a muddy tractor rutted path, and finally onto a surfaced country lane signed toward Wall and the ruins of Leavocetum. Under a tree in the parish graveyard surrounding the ancient church we munched our traditional cemetery picnic: peanut butter and banana sandwiches made with brown granary (real wheat chips) bread. Under the umbrella we hiked the 2 ½ mile footpath to Litchfield, pleased to find the radiator functioning in the Hospital of St. John chapel. We dried out as we rested and prayed in this house of worship founded in 1192. In the hall entrance we read this bit of wisdom painted in white letters on black: "It is admirable to consider how many millions of people come into, and go out of the world, ignorant of themselves, and of the world they have lived in." What is cozier and more English than tea time to refresh the weary? Again we found Egon Ronay's Just a Bite did not let us down. A table for two nestled back beneath the stairwell and beside the heating element was just right for our leisurely pot for two and fancy cakes baked on the premises of Tudor Café in Litchfield House on Bore Street, 250 drizzly yards from the Cathedral. And the payoff for Willard was Alice's decision to get ½ pound of take-home homemade fudge Tudor chocolates for his birthday. Bless her heart! Evensong at 5:30 included a marvelous musical rendition of psalms and anthems by the Cathedral choir school.

MENUS

Menu 1: Epiphany New Year Feast

Course 1—a warming drink with finger appetizers

Course 2—a hearty soup

Course 3—a colorful salad

Course 4—a nourishing plate

Course 5—a memorable end

Epiphany is the first feast of a fresh calendar year—January 6. It comes between the lesser fast of Advent just past and the greater fast of Lent just ahead. Epiphany celebrates the Wise Travelers from the East who followed the light of the Star to find Jesus. For many years a Three Kings Day cake mysteriously appeared at our door on the twelfth day of Christmas. We suspected it was baked and delivered by the Millers, for whom Epiphany overshadows Christmas Day.

Ryan Miller interprets the tradition: "January 6 marks the day the Magi brought gifts—gold, frankincense and myrrh—to the Christ child. We rise early to check on our shoes, which we filled with straw and set on the front porch late last night. The purpose? To feed the kings' camels. In return the kings fill our shoes with trinkets—offerings of gratitude for those who gave sustenance so their weary beasts are able to complete their journey to Bethlehem. We celebrate with a traditional cake with a bean baked in the center. You see, the bean, solid and secret, is the big prize of the morning, and the one who finds it in their breakfast bowl receives honors over the course of the day."

A segment of my recipe and cookbook collections comes from monastic communities and retreat centers where hospitality is foundational, where food almost defines hospitality. In putting together *Heavenly Feasts: Memorable Meals from Monasteries, Abbeys, and Retreats*, Marcia Kelly explained, "Our journeys took us to places of many different spiritual paths, and the food served turned out to be an amazing reflection of the nourishment we were offered at another level. Mealtime blessings are a tradition at many of the places. Pausing a moment to give thanks is a lovely way to begin a meal." One of her favorite prayers before eating makes an appropriate way to begin a New Year feast:

God of pilgrims
Give us always a table to stop at
Where we can tell our story
And sing our song.

The tasting menu below is selected from recipes in this collection with choices for each of the first four courses with the Miller traditional Three Kings Day Cake to end the celebration.

1
Cider Cranberry Hot Toddy
Pennsylvania Railroad Stuffed Celery
Parmesan Stuffed Mushrooms
Down Under Crusty Cheese Cubes

2
Apricot Beef Sweet Sour Soup
OR
Red Potato Carrot Chowder
Guinness Beer Bread with Butter (available throughout the meal)

3
Spinach Pear Salad with Warm Vinaigrette
OR
Endive with Goat Cheese and Walnuts

4
Classic Meatloaf (with ground meats of cook's choice)
OR
Autumn Pork Stew

Either choice served with
Aunt Lucille's Scalloped Potatoes
OR
Corn Leek Bake

And
5-Bean Sweet-Sour Relish
OR
Hawkeye Corn Relish

5
Three Kings Day Cake

Three Kings Day Cake

MAKES: 12 servings

PREP. TIME: 15 minutes

BAKING TIME: 55 minutes

INGREDIENTS:

1 cup butter (2 sticks)

1 ½ cups sugar

2 eggs

1 tsp. orange extract

2 cups + 2 Tbsp. flour

2 tsp. baking powder

¼ tsp. salt

¾ cup orange juice

1. In bowl cream butter with sugar, add eggs one at a time, then add extract.

2. In another bowl mix flour, baking powder, and salt, then add alternately with orange juice to batter.

3. In small Bundt pan, bake in 350˚ oven for 55 minutes. Cool before serving.

Menu 2: St. Valentine's Day Dinner

February 14 is linked with three different Christian martyr saints named Valentine. The first official Saint Valentine's Day was declared in 496 in memory of a third century Roman bishop. Little is known of the other two Valentines, one a Roman priest, the other a missionary in Africa.

Valentine's Day ranks next to Christmas for sending cards. With nostalgia, I remember making and giving cards inscribed with childish love sentiments to all eleven mates in my one-room country school of nine grades each year. As the years passed, childhood exchanges of doggerel ditties gave way to focused expressions toward the one with whom I have shared a lifetime of intimacy.

Inserting a bit of humor into wedding meditations, I often quote a sexist couplet by Anonymous: "Though her kisses always please, what about her recipes?" The most important element in a meal for this day is to choose dishes that use favorite ingredients for the Valentine being honored. It is not the day to be concerned with calories or carbs, but to emphasize love portents (such as chocolate) in whatever form.

In a little more than an hour, the three following dishes can be ready to plate for a tasty, colorful, nutritious main course. But the second and greater course demands more intensive and sustained work, yet well worth the effort to express deep Valentine love.

Fresh Fish Cakes
Roasted Red Potatoes
Wilted Baby Spinach
Boozy Black Forest Cake

Fresh Fish Cakes

MAKES: 6 servings

PREP. TIME: 15 minutes

COOKING TIME: 10 minutes

INGREDIENTS:

8 oz. salmon, poached and flaked

8 oz. crab meat

½ cup panko

3 Tbsp. mayonnaise

1 Tbsp. Dijon mustard

1 Tbsp. fresh parsley, finely chopped

1 Tbsp. fresh dill, finely chopped

1 tsp. salt

½ tsp. pepper

1 Tbsp. olive oil

SAUCE

2 Tbsp. mayonnaise

2 Tbsp. low-fat yogurt

2 Tbsp. lemon juice

1 Tbsp. horseradish, ground

1 Tbsp. fresh parsley, finely chopped

1 Tbsp. sweet pickle relish

½ tsp. sea salt

½ tsp. pepper

1. In bowl, hand mix all ingredients with fingers and form into four cakes.

2. Over moderate heat in skillet fry cakes in oil about 3 minutes on each side until golden brown.

For sauce:

Mix together in small serving bowl.

Roasted Red Potatoes

MAKES: 6 servings

INGREDIENTS:

1 lb. small red potatoes,
    scrubbed and halved

1 quart water

1 tsp. sea salt

1. In saucepan over moderate-low heat cook potatoes just short of soft, about 15 minutes. Drain.

2. Place boiled potatoes in greased 8″ x 8″ pan, spray with olive oil, and sprinkle with sea salt, then roast in 400° oven about 20 minutes.

Wilted Baby Spinach

MAKES: 6 servings

PREP. TIME: 5 minutes

COOKING TIME: 5 minutes

INGREDIENTS:

8 oz. baby spinach

1 Tbsp. olive oil

In skillet over moderate heat wilt spinach in oil for 3 to 5 minutes, stirring occasionally.

Menu 3: Celtic
St. Patrick's Day Lunch

For years on St. Patrick's Day I have worn a green tie from a woolen mill seconds bin in Ireland. One March 17 when I checked in for my daily YMCA routine, the senior volunteer on duty looked at me and said, "You know, Reverend, there are two classes of people in the world: the Irish, and those who wish they were." "You are absolutely right," I replied; "and I'm in second class."

Saint Patrick's story and the Celtic setting inspired and magnetized me long before I first visited Ireland in 1963. And that was only an early morning fueling stop at Shannon in the pre-jet age. I wandered into the terminal lounge at 4 a.m. and was enticed by the refreshment counter's special: Irish coffee. So I ordered one. The lassie asked, "Are you certain you want this so early in the day?" She explained that the distinctive ingredient is not coffee but whiskey. I passed my first opportunity but have enjoyed the Celtic specialty many times since.

We observe the saint's day religiously in our home, usually with guests at our table. Whether lunch or dinner, our menu is chosen from among the recipes below, usually built around either corned beef or lamb stew. Irish soda bread is a must as are pots of strong brewed tea—Bewley's is our house variety. Top off the meal with a colorful green trifle and Paddy's Irish coffee. Consider alternate dishes from other sections of this book as you plan your menu.

Glazed Corned Beef with Carrots and Cabbage
OR
Irish Stew with Indiana Lamb
Colcannon (also called "Champ" or "Bubble and Squeak")
Roasted Parsnip Bread Pudding
Hearty Irish Soda Bread
St. Patrick Trifle
Paddy's Irish Coffee

Glazed Corned Beef with Carrots and Cabbage

MAKES: 8 servings

PREP. TIME: 20 minutes

COOKING TIME: 30 minutes

INGREDIENTS:

3 lbs. corned beef, trimmed

16 oz. lager

2 onions, quartered

2 garlic cloves, quartered

1 cup water

2 bay leaves

6 whole cloves

6 whole peppercorns

1 lb. baby carrots

1 lb. small red potatoes, halved

1 head green cabbage, cut in 8 wedges

GLAZING SAUCE

½ cup whole-grain mustard

½ cup dark brown sugar

1 Tbsp. molasses

3 Tbsp. cider vinegar

1. Place corned beef in Dutch oven. Cover with lager, onions, garlic, water, and spices. Bring to boil over moderate heat, reduce heat, and simmer until tender (about 2 ½ hours).

2. Line 9″ x 14″ baking pan with foil. With tongs, place corned beef on sheet.

3. Add carrots, potatoes, and cabbage to juice in Dutch oven and simmer, covered, until veggies are almost tender (10–12 minutes).

4. In bowl combine mustard, brown sugar, molasses, and vinegar. Brush corned beef with 2 Tbsp. of glaze. Roast corned beef at 375˚ for 15 minutes; remove from baking sheet and slice thinly.

5. Serve with veggies and remaining sauce.

Irish Stew with Indiana Lamb

MAKES: 8 servings

PREP. TIME: 30 minutes

COOKING TIME: 3 hours

INGREDIENTS:

- 3 lbs. Indiana lamb stew meat, trimmed and cut in 1 in. chunks
- 1 lb. potatoes, scrubbed and quartered
- 1 lb. carrots, scrubbed and cut in 2 in. chunks
- 1 lb. yellow onions, peeled and quartered
- 4 Tbsp. fresh parsley, chopped
- 2 cups water
- 1 tsp. salt
- 1 tsp. pepper
- 1 lb. frozen peas

PARSLEY SAUCE

- 2 Tbsp. Irish butter
- 1 Tbsp. onion, finely chopped
- 2 Tbsp. flour
- ¾ cup half and half
- 1 Tbsp. fresh parsley, finely chopped
- 1 tsp. English mustard
- 1 tsp. nutmeg
- ½ tsp. salt
- 1 tsp. pepper

1. Put all ingredients except peas in ovenproof Dutch oven; stir, cover, and bring to simmer over medium heat.

2. Transfer to 250° oven; bake until lamb is almost tender (about 2 hours).

3. Remove Dutch oven from oven, stir in peas, and return to oven for 20 minutes more.

4. Remove stew from oven to sit for 20 minutes before serving in individual bowls. Remove ¼ cup of liquid and set aside for sauce.

5. Meanwhile, make sauce. Melt butter in small skillet over medium heat. Add onions and cook for a minute. Whisk in flour and cook until golden, about a minute. Whisk in reserved liquid from stew (up to ¼ cup), half and half, parsley, and spices, whisking until thickened, about five minutes. Serve sauce in gravy pitcher for passing.

Colcannon (also called "Champ" or "Bubble and Squeak")

MAKES: 8 servings

PREP. TIME: 20 minutes

COOKING TIME: 25 minutes

Living in Ireland for six months as volunteer workers, we learned that colcannon is at the top of the comfort food charts, and no surprise since rural families stored potatoes and cabbage for year-round use. Every family has its own favorite recipe variation—experiment and find your family's favorite.

INGREDIENTS:

- 3–3 ½ lbs. potatoes (russets preferred), peeled and cut into chunks
- 4–6 Tbsp. butter
- 4 Tbsp. salt, divided
- 4 cups cabbage, chopped (or other leafy green, such as kale)
- 5 or 6 green onions, minced, including onion greens
- 1 ¼ cups milk

1. Cover potatoes with cold water, and add 3 tsp. salt. Boil until soft, 15–20 minutes. Drain in colander.

2. In same cooking pot, melt butter. Add cabbage and cook until wilted, 5–6 minutes. Add onion and cook 2 minutes longer.

3. Add milk and cooked potatoes, reducing heat to low. With potato masher, mash potatoes, mixing with cabbage and onion, adding 1 tsp. salt. Serve hot.

Option: Drizzle more butter over top of colcannon before serving.

Roasted Parsnip Bread Pudding

MAKES: 8 servings

PREP. TIME: 20 minutes

BAKING TIME: 75 minutes

INGREDIENTS:

1 lb. parsnips, scrubbed and cut into ½ in pieces

1 Tbsp. olive oil

2 tsp. sea salt *divided*

1 tsp. pepper *divided*

8 Tbsp. butter (1 stick) *divided*

2 leeks, white and pale green parts cleaned, halved, and thinly sliced

½ cup dry white wine

2 Tbsp. fresh thyme, finely chopped

6 eggs

1 cup half and half

1 cup yogurt

1 cup hard cheese of choice, shredded *divided*

16 oz. day-old bread of choice, torn in pieces

1. Arrange parsnips on greased baking sheet, drizzle with oil, season with half the salt and pepper, and roast in 425° oven until caramelized, about 25 minutes. Stir several times during roasting. Remove from oven. Reduce heat to 375°.

2. In medium pan over medium heat, heat 2 Tbs. butter and sauté leeks until almost tender, about 5 minutes. Remove from heat, add wine and return to heat. Simmer 1 to 2 minutes. Add thyme. Remove from heat and stir in roasted parsnips.

3. In large bowl whisk together 3 Tbsp. melted butter, eggs, half and half, yogurt, and remaining salt and pepper. Stir in ¾ cup cheese. Add leek and parsnip mixture and fold in bread chunks.

4. Pour in greased 9" x 14" baking dish, cover loosely with foil, and bake in preheated 375° oven until golden brown, about 45 minutes. Remove foil, sprinkle with remaining cheese, and return to oven for 15 more minutes. Let stand at least 5 minutes before serving.

Tip: To make ahead, mixture can be refrigerated overnight; let stand at room temperature 15 minutes before baking.

Menu 4: Shrove Tuesday New Orleans Supper

In January 2006 Alice and I chose to overnight in St. Martinville, Louisiana, home of Henry Wadsorth Longfellow's "Evangeline." After checking in to our B&B, we walked across the street to the Cultural Heritage Center where a poster announced: A TASTE OF CREOLE *HERE TOMORROW NIGHT 6 P.M.* I quickly returned to our host, requesting another 24 hours to take advantage of this serendipity car travel makes possible.

The five courses hosted by Chef Victor Montoya introduced us to legendary Louisiana and New Orleans cuisine and cooking "and the evolution of this art form firmly rooted in the historic pathways of this colorful city and state,"(in the words of archivist Gerald Patout before we ate). To further whet appetites, diners could peruse menus while waiting in the buffet line:

Appetizer. *Fresh Dungeness crab cakes, Italian cheeses, roast corn and peppers prepared with a fusion of French and Italian cuisine; accentuated with a classic burr blanc lemon butter sauce.*
Salad. *Grilled eggplant and tri-colored sweet bell peppers with marinated portabella mushroom on top of a seasonal medley of greens complemented with a chipotle basil aioli.*
Soup. *Fresh lobster bisque with a mirepoix base, cream and seasoning accompanied with cheese toast points—a must try!*
Entrée. *Pork tenderloin medallion stuffed with seasoned Italian breadcrumbs, cheese, pine nuts and pancetta bacon slow roasted to perfect consistency by our own resident chefs served with a brown demi-glaze.*
Dessert. *Seasonal fruit torta. This variation of the traditional torta is a work of art! The best way to end your evening with us. Covered with a chocolate dome, served with a sweet crème Blanc and strawberry sauce.*

In New Orleans, Shrove Tuesday ends the season of Mardi Gras—the colorful and oft raucous celebration between Epiphany and the beginning of Lent on Ash Wednesday. Recipes for this festive supper come from my course of study in Cajun and Creole cooking in the New Orleans School of Cooking in February 2003. My certificate declares "the recipient of this diploma demonstrated a knowledge and appreciation of real food, possesses the skills and 'joie de vivre' necessary for the faithful reproduction of Louisiana's culinary gifts to the world." Instructor Michael underscored that there can be no mistakes in cooking unless the cook admits it to be a mistake—wise words I find to be of continuing comfort.

Red Jambalaya
Mixed Greens Salad Medley with Fresh Clementine Segments and Nuts
Bourbon Street Bread Pudding
Pecan Pralines
Hot Drinks of Choice

Red Jambalaya
(meaning "rice with a surprise")

MAKES: 10 servings

PREP. TIME: 30 minutes

COOKING TIME: 40 minutes

INGREDIENTS:

¼ cup oil, divided

1 chicken, cooked and boned

1 tsp. salt

1 tsp. pepper

1 ½ lb. spiced stuffed sausage, sliced in ½ in pieces

1 ½ Tbsp. brown sugar

2 garlic cloves, chopped

¼ cup sweet Hungarian paprika

4 cups onions, chopped

2 cups celery, chopped

2 cups green peppers, chopped

1 Tbsp. Creole seasoning [or make your own: 1 tsp. each of oregano, thyme, allspice, and black pepper]

2 bay leaves

5 cups liquid (any combination of water, vegetable juice, stock)

4 cups long grain rice

1 cup cherry tomatoes, halved

1 cup green onions, chopped

1. In pot over medium heat brown chicken and seasonings in ⅛ cup oil. Add sausage and sauté with chicken. Remove meat from pot.

2. Heat remaining oil, stir in brown sugar, and caramelize. Add garlic and paprika. Stir in the vegetable trinity (onion, celery, green pepper) and sauté until tender.

3. Return meat to pot, add Creole seasoning, and stir in liquid. Bring to boil. Add rice and return to boil. Cover and simmer; after 10 minutes remove cover and quickly turn rice from top to bottom completely. Add tomatoes and green onions. Simmer another 15 minutes. Serve.

Tip: Use 1 ¼ cup liquid for 1 cup rice to feed three; overseason to compensate for absorption

Salad Medley of Mixed Greens with Fresh Clementine Segments

MAKES: 10 servings

PREP. TIME: 15 minutes

INGREDIENTS:

16 oz. mixed salad greens

2 Tbsp. blood tangerine Balsamic vinegar

2 Tbsp. blood orange olive oil

3 clementines, peeled and segmented

¼ cup mixed nuts, chopped and toasted

In large salad serving bowl, mix greens with vinegar and oil thoroughly. Arrange clementine segments on top and sprinkle with nuts.

Bourbon Street Bread Pudding

MAKES: 10 servings

PREP. TIME: 15 minutes

BAKING TIME: 75 minutes

INGREDIENTS:

8 cups stale bread, crumbled (the better the bread, the better the pudding)

1 cup sugar

1 cup brown sugar

¼ cup cinnamon

2 tsp. nutmeg

3 eggs, whisked

8 Tbsp. (1 stick) butter, melted

4 cups milk

1 Tbsp. vanilla

RAISINS AND NUTS (OPTIONAL):

1 cup raisins, soaked in ⅓ cup of strong coffee, tea or liquor

1 cup pecans, chopped

1 cup coconut, shredded.

WARM BOURBON SAUCE:

8 Tbsp. (1 stick) butter

1 ½ cup confectioners sugar

2 egg yolks

⅓ cup bourbon

1. Combine dry ingredients in large bowl. Whisk together eggs, butter, milk and vanilla. Stir wet ingredients into dry ingredients (if using raisins and/or nuts, incorporate them into the pudding at this point). Mixture should be very moist but not soupy.

2. Pour into 9″ x 13″ (or larger) baking dish. Bake at 350° for 75 minutes, until top is golden brown. Serve warm with warm Bourbon sauce.

For sauce:

1. In small pan over medium heat cream butter and confectioners sugar until butter is absorbed.

2. Remove from heat and blend in egg yolks. Pour in bourbon gradually, stirring constantly. Sauce will thicken as it cools.

Tip: Substitute your favorite liqueur or fruit juice for bourbon for a variety of sauces to complement your bread pudding.

Pecan Pralines

MAKES: 10 servings

PREP. TIME: 15 minutes

COOKING TIME: 15 minutes

INGREDIENTS:

1 cup sugar

1 cup brown sugar

1 tsp. baking soda

1 cup buttermilk

2 Tbsp. butter

2 cups pecan halves

½ cup perfect pecan halves

1. In large saucepan, boil sugars, baking soda, and buttermilk until it reaches 210° on candy thermometer. Stir frequently to scrape bottom and sides.

2. Add butter and 2 cups pecans. Cook, stirring constantly to 230° (or until mixture forms a soft ball when dropped in cold water). Remove from heat, cool 1 minute. With wooden spoon beat until thickened and creamy.

3. Drop by tablespoonfuls onto waxed paper. Dot tops with perfect pecan halves.

Creole cooks spared no lengths to achieve perfection in making candy, Instructor Michael said, as he put together the praline ingredients. Along with their vast collection of recipes, Creoles had their own secret methods for making the best pralines, which they guarded and handed down through the generations. Pralines get their name from Marshal Luplesis-Praslin (1598–1695) whose butler's recipe for sugar-coated almonds was heralded as an effective 17th century digestive aid. When French colonists settled Louisiana, cooks substituted native pecans for almonds, hence pralines.

Menu 5: Agape Bible Lands Breakfast

Fish Pâté with Sesame Crisps
Vegetable Juice with Lemon Slices
Eggs Indienne
Whole Grain Bread of Choice with Herb Jelly
Kidron Melon Mousse
Cardamom Cakes
Blue Mountain Coffee or Irish Breakfast Tea

On an August Saturday morning, I prepared breakfast for eight disciples on the shores of Lake Wawasee in Kosiasko County, Indiana. As I did so, I remembered Jesus once did the same before he spoke his final farewell to those in his inner circle. *Loaves and Fishes: Foods from Bible Times* by Malvina Kinard and Janet Crisler inspired my menu.

Fish Pâté

INGREDIENTS:

12–16 oz. fresh wild caught salmon filets

32 oz. fresh filet of sole or other white fish

4 egg whites

1 ½ cups whipping cream

3 Tbsp. fresh dill chopped

1 tsp. salt

⅛ tsp. white pepper

⅛ tsp. red pepper

Cucumber and lemon slices for garnish

1. Remove skin from salmon and cut in two strips; set aside.

2. Cut sole in 1-inch chunks; blend small amounts in blender or processor with egg whites one at a time until smooth. Put in bowl set over a bowl of ice.

3. Gradually beat in cream until texture is fine; season with dill, salt, and pepper.

4. Spoon half the mixture into buttered 9″ x 5″ x 3″ glass loaf pan; place salmon slices in center and cover with remaining sole mixture. Cover with buttered parchment paper.

5. Set loaf pan in pan of hot water in 350° oven for 45 minutes.

6. Chill thoroughly before serving. Garnish with cucumber and lemon slices.

Sesame Crisps

INGREDIENTS:

1 cup flour

1 cup whole-wheat flour

¾ cup butter, broken in walnut-sized pieces

3 Tbsp. ice water (more if needed)

1 cup sesame seeds, toasted

1. Combine flours with butter using fingers to rub together until texture resembles cornmeal.

2. Add ice water to make cohesive dough; mix in seeds.

3. Chill for 30–45 minutes, and then roll dough out thin on lightly floured board.

4. Cut into desired shapes and bake on greased sheet in 325° oven until crisp, about 15 minutes.

Eggs Indienne (seasoned East Indian style)

INGREDIENTS:

8 eggs, hard boiled

¼ cup mayonnaise

¼ cup yogurt

2 Tbsp. half and half

1 Tbsp. tomato paste

2 tsp. curry powder

½ tsp. salt

¼ tsp. pepper

¼ cup sweet pickle relish

2 Tbsp. fresh parsley, chopped finely

1 tsp. paprika

1. Peel and halve eggs. Remove yolks to bowl and mash fine with fork.

2. Mix in other ingredients in order (except parsley and paprika), stirring with each addition until smooth.

3. Spoon and mound yolk mixture into egg white halves. Arrange on serving plate garnished with parsley sprigs. Sprinkle with paprika.

Herb Jelly

INGREDIENTS:

1 cup fresh herb leaves (rosemary, tarragon, mint)

1 ½ cups boiling water

5 cups sugar

1 cup cider vinegar

8 oz. pectin

Green food coloring

1. Cover leaves with boiling water; add sugar and vinegar, stirring to dissolve, then boil 10 min.
2. Strain through a cheesecloth; add pectin and a few drops of green coloring.
3. Pour into sterile hot glasses and seal.

Kidron Melon Mousse

INGREDIENTS:

2 cups ripe cantaloupe, mashed or blended

⅓ cup sugar

1 envelope plain gelatin

¼ cup cold water

1 Tbsp. fresh lemon or lime juice

1 cup whipping cream

1 tsp. vanilla extract

1. Combine cantaloupe and sugar; heat until sugar is dissolved.
2. Soften gelatin in water then add to warm fruit to dissolve; add juice.
3. Whip cream, add vanilla, and fold into gelatin mixture.
4. Spoon into eight glass dessert dishes; chill thoroughly before serving with a garnish of a fresh seasonal fruit.

Cardamom Cakes

INGREDIENTS:

1 cup flour

¾ cup whole-wheat flour

1 tsp. baking soda

¼ tsp. salt

1 tsp. ground cardamom

1 tsp. ground cinnamon

½ tsp. ground nutmeg

2 eggs

¾ cup sugar

¼ cup olive oil

½ cup yogurt

½ cup prune sauce

1 tsp. vanilla extract

Zest of one orange

½ cup pistachio nuts, chopped

2 Tbsp. confectioners sugar

1. In bowl combine flours, soda, salt, and spices.

2. In another bowl beat eggs with sugar and oil. Gradually add flour mixture alternately with yogurt and prune sauce. Stir in vanilla, orange zest, and nuts.

3. Divide in 12 portions in greased cupcake pan. Bake at 375° for about 25 minutes, testing until toothpick comes out clean. Remove from oven; cool 5 minutes before loosening with knife. Sprinkle with confectioners sugar before serving warm.

Menu 6: Autumn Thanksgiving Meal

Thanksgiving is a word and a reality with varying meanings. Americans most naturally think of the holiday each fourth Thursday in November proclaimed by a president who also pardons a turkey. Canadians celebrate a month earlier. All I ever learned about Thanksgiving in kindergarten I now know to be more fiction than fact. Yes, the three-day celebration in 1621 included both Pilgrims and Wampanoag. But the next American thanksgiving observance in 1676 excluded Indians as colonists celebrated victory over the "heathen natives."

When our family lived in Ghana we joined our African church sisters and brothers for thanksgiving harvests—a time in the tropical autumn to gather fruits of the farm for a fundraiser. In temporary chapels with palm-branch roofs we sang choruses, danced our offerings to the communion table, and prayed long thanksgiving prayers simultaneously and aloud. Like the Psalmist, "These things I remember, how I went with the throng and led them in procession to the house of God, with glad shouts and songs of thanksgiving, a multitude keeping festival" (Psalm 42:4).

This menu combines both traditional and non-traditional dishes for an easily prepared family meal that makes an attractive and nourishing table.

Wild Salmon Pâté Ball
Baked Sour Cream Chicken with Dressing
OR
Roast of Choice
English Yorkshire Pudding
Orange Cranberry Salad
Copper Pennies
Blueberry Buckle

Wild Salmon Pâté Ball

MAKES: 12 servings

PREP. TIME: 10 minutes

INGREDIENTS:

15-oz. can wild caught salmon

3 oz. fat-free cream cheese

2 Tbsp. fresh onion grated

1 Tbsp. fresh horseradish

1 Tbsp. fresh lemon juice

1 tsp. Worcestershire sauce

¼ cup pecans, finely chopped

¼ cup fresh parsley, finely chopped

1. Wash hands and mix all ingredients (except pecans and parsley) until fully blended; form into a ball.

2. Chill for at least an hour; roll in pecans and parsley. Serve with cook's cracker choice.

Baked Sour Cream Chicken with Dressing

MAKES: 6 servings

PREP. TIME: 30 minutes

COOKING TIME: 90 minutes

Mother Minnie Wenger Roth's start-from-scratch use of a stewing bird.

INGREDIENTS:

1 stewing chicken (about five pounds)

14 oz. can mushroom soup

1 cup sour cream

4 oz. can sliced mushrooms

6 oz. package stuffing mix

14 oz. can chicken broth

1 onion, chopped

2 cups celery, chopped

1 Tbsp. butter

1. In pan stew chicken over medium heat until well cooked and meat comes off bones easily. Save broth. Debone when sufficiently cool and cut meat in small pieces. Place chicken in greased 9″ x 13″ baking pan.

2. In bowl mix soup, sour cream, and undrained mushrooms. Spread over chicken.

3. In same bowl, combine stuffing mix and broth.

4. In pan sauté onion and celery in butter over medium heat. Add stuffing mix and broth. Spread over chicken mixture. Bake at 325° for 40 minutes.

English Yorkshire Pudding

MAKES: 12 servings

PREP. TIME: 10 minutes

RESTING TIME: 1 hour

BAKING TIME: 20–30 minutes

An English Sunday pub roast by definition comes with the traditional Yorkshire pudding, although not really a pudding by American definition. But it is a mighty tasty accompaniment to a chef-carved thanksgiving roast of choice: beef, chicken, ham, nut, or turkey.

INGREDIENTS:

½ cup flour

2 eggs

½ tsp. salt

1 cup milk (divided, ¼ + ¾)

¼ cup butter

1. Sift flour into bowl; make well in center for eggs, salt, and ¼ cup of milk.

2. Beat gradually until smooth, adding rest of milk as mixture blends. (Alternatively, use a blender at top speed). Chill for 1 hour.

3. Put an 8″ x 8″ pan into 425° oven with butter.

4. When very hot, add chilled batter after stirring several times. Check after 20 minutes for crisp, brown top; may take 10–15 minutes longer. Serve with meat of choice.

Copper Pennies

MAKES: 8 servings

PREPARATION: 20 minutes

RESTING: overnight

A common midwestern recipe I learned at my first cooking school from the late Loretta Lovejoy, owner of the Patchwork Quilt Bed and Breakfast near Middlebury, Indiana.

INGREDIENTS:

5 carrots, sliced

1 tsp. salt

1 onion, sliced thin

1 green pepper, diced

SAUCE

15-oz. can tomato soup

½ cup vegetable oil

¾ cup vinegar

¾ cup sugar

1 tsp. Worcestershire sauce

2 tsp. prepared mustard

1. Cook carrots in salted water until tender but not soft. Drain and cool. Combine carrots with other uncooked vegetables in glass baking dish.

2. Combine ingredients for sauce and pour over prepared vegetables. Mix until vegetables are well-coated.

3. Marinate overnight. Serve chilled.

Blueberry Buckle

MAKES: 8 servings

PREP. TIME: 15 minutes

BAKING TIME: 45 minutes

Inspired by a recipe from my cousin Donna Swartzendruber, daughter of Aunt Lucille.

INGREDIENTS:

½ cup olive oil

½ cup sugar

1 egg, beaten

1 cup flour

1 cup whole-wheat flour

2 ½ tsp. baking powder

¼ tsp. salt

½ cup milk

2 cups blueberries, fresh or frozen

TOPPING

½ cup brown sugar

½ cup flour

1 tsp. ground cinnamon

¼ cup butter

1. In bowl combine oil, sugar, and egg; beat until fluffy.

2. Sift dry ingredients together. Add alternately with milk and egg mixture.

3. Spread evenly in greased 11" x 17" baking pan. Cover with berries.

4. To make topping, cut together brown sugar, flour, cinnamon, and butter. Sprinkle over berries.

5. Bake at 350° for 45 minutes. Serve warm with vanilla frozen dessert of choice.

Menu 7: Advent Tea

Advent begins four Sundays before Christmas as a countdown to the world's most celebrated holy day. Two traditions at our house provide seasonal ritual, a calendar and a wreath. The Advent calendar has thirty-one camouflaged windows opened day by day as a family prayer is spoken. The Advent wreath of evergreen twigs has four candles (preferably three purple and a pink) lighted Sunday by Sunday, as a part of the Advent scripture story is read. On Christmas Eve, the white Christ candle in the wreath's center is lighted, the familiar Christmas story is read, and each family member selects a psalm chosen randomly from 150 numbers in the Psalm Bag (a Roth tradition handed down from the Old Country).

For Christians, Advent is the season that invites hospitality—an intentional time to anticipate, to prepare, to wait for visitors both expected and unexpected. That preparation includes making and storing candies and cookies. A pantry of home-kitchen goodies along with festive decorations throughout the house equals a call for hospitality. Advent includes the year's longest nights so setting out a candlelight tea for friends old and new is a wonderful opportunity to lighten winter dark.

Alice's Scones
Holy Scripture Cake with Butter Brown Frosting
Old English Syllabub
Sherry-Sugared Walnuts
Hot and Cold Drinks of Choice

Alice's Scones

MAKES: 8 servings

PREP. TIME: 20 minutes

BAKING TIME: 12 minutes

INGREDIENTS:

1 ¼ cups rolled oats

¾ cup all-purpose flour

¾ cup whole wheat pastry flour

⅓ cup sugar

1 Tbsp. baking powder

½ tsp. baking soda

⅛ tsp. salt

½ cup currants

2 Tbsp. butter, melted

1 egg, lightly beaten

⅓ cup Greek yogurt

1. In large bowl, stir together oats, flours, sugar, baking powder, baking soda, and salt. Stir in currants and make a well in center of dry ingredients.

2. Combine butter, egg, and yogurt; add to dry ingredients, stirring just until moistened.

3. Turn onto lightly floured surface and gently knead several times to form a ball. Pat ball into 8-inch circle, cut this into 8 wedges. Place wedges on lightly oiled baking sheet.

4. In 425 degree oven bake about 12 minutes, until firm to the touch. Transfer to rack to cool slightly. Serve warm.

Holy Scripture Cake with Butter Brown Frosting

This culinary curiosity has been around for a long time among devoted Bible lovers. To simplify the recipe for less literate biblical readers, ingredients are translated with common names. The frosting recipe comes from my sister Karen Roth Watson.

MAKES: 16 servings

BIBLICAL RESEARCH TIME: 30 minutes

PREP. TIME: 20 minutes

BAKING TIME: 90 minutes

INGREDIENTS:

1 cup Judges 5:25 (butter)

1 cup Jeremiah 6:20 (sugar)

3 Isaiah 10:14 (eggs)

3 cups 1 Kings 4:22 (flour)

2 tsp. Luke 13:21 (baking powder)

½ tsp. Leviticus 2:13 (salt)

3 tsp. 1 Kings 10:10 (cinnamon, nutmeg, cloves)

½ cup Judges 4:19 (milk)

1 Tbsp. Proverbs 24:13 (honey)

2 cups 1 Samuel 30:12, chopped (figs, raisins)

½ cup Genesis 43:11, chopped (almonds, pistachio nuts)

BUTTER BROWN FROSTING

½ cup butter

2 cups confectioners sugar

3–5 Tbsp. boiling water

1 tsp. vanilla extract

1. In bowl cream Judges 5:25 with Jeremiah 6:20 until fluffy. Add Isaiah 10:14 and beat together one at a time.

2. In another bowl combine 1 Kings 4:22, Luke 13:21, Leviticus 2:13 and 1 Kings 10:10. Mix into first bowl alternately with Judges 4:19. Add Proverbs 24:13 and mix well.

3. Stir in 1 Samuel 30:12 and Genesis 43:11. Transfer mixture into greased and floured Bundt pan. Bake at 325° for about 75 minutes, or until a toothpick comes out clean. Remove from oven, cool 5 minutes, lightly loosen edges with knife and turn upside down on baking rack until fully cool before frosting.

Over medium heat melt butter in saucepan and cook, stirring constantly, until butter stops bubbling and is nut-brown in color (*warning: do not scorch*). Remove from heat and add confectioners sugar, boiling water, and vanilla. Beat until smooth, and spread on cake. *Adjust amounts of sugar and water for desired consistency.*

Old English Syllabub

MAKES: 6 servings

PREP. TIME: 15 minutes

I was introduced to syllabub in Gran Canaria in 1971 on a mandated mid-term leave from a mission assignment in tropical Africa. It delighted my palate and the maker's rather complex recipe went home with me. But like many other intentions of life, I neglected to ever use it. Recently I uncovered this simpler way to make this Old English white wine pudding.

INGREDIENTS:

2 cups whipping cream

⅔ cup sugar

1 Tbsp. vanilla extract

½ cup semi-dry white wine

¼ cup fresh lemon juice

¼ cup dry sherry

12 maraschino cherries, 6 red, 6 green

1. In medium bowl whip cream until small peaks form (not until stiff).

2. Mix in sugar, vanilla, wine, lemon juice, and sherry (in order) just until combined.

3. Spoon evenly into 6 small stemmed wine glasses. Top each with a red and green cherry. Serve immediately.

Sherry-Sugared Walnuts

MAKES: 1 quart

PREP. TIME: 10 minutes

COOKING TIME: 5 minutes

DRYING TIME: 15 minutes

An irresistible crunchy-munchy to nibble before, during, and after drinks of choice.

INGREDIENTS:

¼ cup sherry

1 cup brown sugar

1 tsp. pumpkin-pie spice

¼ tsp. salt

3 Tbsp. light corn syrup

4 cups walnut halves

¼ cup sugar

1. In pan over medium heat blend sherry, brown sugar, spice, salt, and syrup.

2. Stir in nuts, mixing until coated. Remove from heat.

3. Put sugar in clean bowl and mix in nuts until they have taken on as much sugar as they can.

4. Spread on baking sheet to dry. Store in airtight container until used.

Eight decades as host and guest at home and away

1983–1992

While leading a tour group I found this bit of doggerel in *A Merry Go Round of Recipes from Jamaica*: "We may live without friends, we may live without books, but civilized humans, cannot live without cooks." *Some Icelandic Recipes* came from a Reykjavik bookstore during a 48-hour stopover in 1984. I got the *Southwestern Indian Recipe Book* (from Apache, Pima, Papago, Pueblo, and Navajo native peoples) on a 1983 visit to northeastern Arizona.

One of the most expensive meals I have enjoyed was a 1984 anniversary dinner in Vianden, Luxembourg at Restaurant Mont Saint Nicolas when Alice and I were given a gratuity by Tourmagination. I couldn't carry the handwritten menu board with me so I only remember the final course—a dessert sampler consumed with great gusto.

In August 1988 we hosted two Irish teas for friends in groups of 8 using the same menu:

Irish Sparkler (white grape juice with lemon soda and pretzel rings)
Salad Platter (on leaf lettuce: cucumber, green pepper, zucchini, green beans, and onions, with cauliflower marinated in olive oil and wine vinegar)
Irish Soda Bread with Homemade Butter and Apple Butter
Seafood Mousse
Irish Cheese Board of Farmhouse Cheeses with Jacobs Crackers and White Grapes
    Cooleeney Camembert (Moyne, Thurles)
    Keenogue (McCullough)
    Carrigbyrne St. Killian, soft (Wexford)
    Lough Caume, goat (Clare)
Scones and Blueberry Jelly
Bewley's Leaf Tea
Irish Emerald Mist, decaff
After Eight Mints

RECIPES
FROM
FRIENDS

Chef Adam Roth

Adam Roth, *Executive Chef*
SaddleRidge Restaurant at Beaver Creek, Colorado

Never forget your secret ingredient.

It all started as a toddler in Iowa with a memory I don't have, but one that my Grandmother often tells me. I sat on her lap kneading dough with my tiny hands—one can say my culinary journey started there. Growing up I saw what an integral part food played in my family. Going to grandparents for holiday celebrations, we could always depend on the same delicious dishes. They never changed much, but were always perfectly prepared with lots of love. Love was the secret ingredient. Sensing how food made everyone happy, I started cooking at home more, for myself and my own family, making ridiculous dishes and testing my parents' patience. Grilled Cornish Game Hen, that was me at age twelve (ask my parents if it was any good).

When old enough to work legally I turned to a local hotel for my first job: washing dishes. At fourteen, I began to see what a professional kitchen was really about: fast and loud with activity always going on, stereo music playing, and an occasional practical joke—every day was the same, yet very different and always full of new challenges. Moving up in the restaurant world, I went from dish washer to fry cook. This opened my eyes to what we call The Rush: when everyone comes in to eat at seven o'clock. You can't slow down—just have to work faster, but don't fry your fingers off! It was like getting ready for a game every night. The practice: prepping food. Pre-game warm ups: the early diners. Game time: the rush. Post-game interviews: clean-up time (the faster you clean, the sooner you can go home). All this, followed by making your prep list for tomorrow. Every day is like that, but when you don't know how many people are coming in or what they will order, each day presents new challenges. That is what I love about the professional kitchen.

After cutting teeth in the world of fast and loud, I knew that culinary school and the chef life was for me. I moved to Denver, Colorado for culinary school in 2001. I always loved Colorado; this is when I fell in love with snowboarding, too. With some of the world's best ski resorts and clientele, Colorado mountains also offer some of the world's finest restaurants. So after graduating, I moved to Vail Valley to pursue my love of snowboarding and continue my education working in Vail's upscale restaurants.

After seven years in the Valley, working my way up the chain of command, I am now Executive Chef at SaddleRidge in Beaver Creek. Nestled slope side in Beaver Creek, SaddleRidge is the country's largest private collection of Western and Native American artifacts. Here I hone my skills creating Southwest-inspired steakhouse fare, always prepared with love and patience. You may think that my day would be focused on cooking; rather, like a head coach, my day revolves around creating the "game plan." Creating menus, developing budgets, ordering food, scheduling deliveries, writing standard recipes, scheduling cooks, talking to guests, making TV appearances—these parts of my game plan are what it takes to keep the professional kitchen winning. But the most important part of my job is coaching players: teaching my cooks good techniques and turning them into professional chefs, just like my mentors did on my journey.

Although you may not be on a vocational path to executive chef, hopefully I can teach you something with my recipes. But above all, never forget your secret ingredient—lots of love.

Roasted Brussels Sprouts with Bacon, Pecans, and Goat Cheese

MAKES: 8 servings

PREP. TIME: 15 minutes

ROASTING TIME: 15 minutes

I learned in culinary school that roasting vegetables at high heat caramelizes natural sugars and creates a unique flavor you can't get from boiling or steaming. For an easy side dish, try this technique with almost any vegetable; broccoli, green beans, or carrots are all good choices.

INGREDIENTS:

1 lb. Brussels sprouts

2 slices bacon, cooked and crumbled, 1 Tbsp. fat reserved

1 Tbsp. olive oil

Salt and pepper to taste

¼ cup pecans, toasted and roughly chopped

2 oz. Chevre goat cheese

1. With a paring knife, remove root ends of Brussels sprouts. Remove any outer discolored leaves and cut each sprout in half. While cleaning the sprouts place a sheet tray in a 450° oven.

2. Put halved sprouts in a mixing bowl, and toss with the reserved bacon fat and olive oil. Season with salt and pepper, being careful with salt as bacon fat is quite salty.

3. Take hot sheet tray from oven and spread sprouts in a single layer. Roast for 8–14 minutes, depending on size, until a sharp knife pierces them easily.

4. Place in serving dish and top with bacon, pecans, and goat cheese.

Apple Cider Brine for Pork or Chicken

PREP. TIME: 15 minutes

CHILLING: 30 minutes

MARINATING: 4–24 hours

Often times chicken or pork can become overly dry too easily. Brining is a simple technique to ensure your lean cuts do not dry out while cooking, and also to enhance flavor.

INGREDIENTS:

2 cups water

½ cup brown sugar

½ cup kosher salt

4 cups apple cider

2 cups ice

¼ cup apple cider vinegar

1 cinnamon stick

6 whole cloves

2 garlic cloves, crushed

1. Bring water to a boil in pan. Remove from heat and add brown sugar and salt. Stir. Once dissolved, add remaining ingredients, again stirring until the ice melts. Refrigerate until completely chilled.

2. At this point the brine is ready to use. Place chicken pieces or cut pork chops in brine for 4 hours then cook as usual. For whole poultry birds or whole pork loins, brine overnight up to 24 hours.

Cherry Cola Steak Sauce

PREP. TIME: 15 minutes

COOKING TIME: 1 hour

Many commercial steak sauces rely on raisins for sweetness and body. This sauce uses dry cherries instead, and adds an unexpected twist with the addition of cherry cola. Use this as a steak sauce or a finishing BBQ sauce for grilled meats.

INGREDIENTS:

1 Tbsp. olive oil

1 clove garlic, chopped

½ white onion, chopped

1 cup ketchup

1 lemon (juice only)

½ cup cider vinegar

2 Tbsp. soy sauce

2 Tbsp. brown sugar

1 Tbsp. Dijon mustard

1 cup dried cherries

16 oz. cherry cola

1 tsp. black pepper

1. Heat oil in sauce pot over medium heat. Sweat garlic and onion in oil until soft. Add remaining ingredients. Simmer one hour.

2. Remove from heat and let cool slightly. Add mixture to blender or food processor and puree until smooth.

Macadamia Nut Brittle

MAKES: 24 servings

PREP. TIME: 20 minutes

COOKING TIME: 40 minutes

Making peanut brittle with my Grandfather Royce Roth is one of my best childhood memories. This recipe substitutes peanuts with the rich and buttery Macadamia nut. Any nut could be substituted in this recipe; cashews, pine nuts, or even pistachios are all excellent choices.

INGREDIENTS:

1 ¼ cups sugar

⅓ cup light corn syrup

⅓ cup water

8 oz. unsalted butter

1 tsp. salt

½ tsp. baking soda

2 cups Macadamia nuts, toasted and roughly chopped

1. In medium sauce pot add sugar, corn syrup and water. Bring to boil over medium heat. Boil 3 to 4 minutes, cover pot with aluminum foil, and boil 5 more minutes. Remove foil, add butter, and cook for 30 minutes, or until a candy thermometer reaches 300°, stirring occasionally.

2. While sugar mixture is cooking, cover a half sheet pan with wax paper and grease thoroughly. Have a slender metal spatula greased and ready as well. When sugar reaches temperature, stir in salt, baking soda, and nuts. Immediately spread the nut mixture onto the greased sheet pan, and spread as thinly as possible with the spatula.

3. Cool completely and break into pieces.

Chef Adam Williams

Adam Williams, *Chef and Co-owner*
Adam's Bistro and Catering, Elkhart, Indiana

Mother's love of food rubbed off.

From childhood I knew I was going to be a chef and own a restaurant. I admit that seemed a tall order growing up in Shelby, Mississippi, where half of the town's three thousand people live in poverty. But Mother's love of food rubbed off. She worked in the restaurant business and sent me to apprentice with friends around the South who ran eateries. After high school I attended culinary school in Biloxi, graduating at the top of my class.

Although I had some rough times along the way, my childhood dream was realized in 2006 when my wife Maggie and I opened Unique Blends in the neighborhood where we live in Elkhart and Adam's Bistro two years later.

The food business, like Maggie's grandparents' Elkhart County farm, is a family affair. Adam's Bistro and Catering involves our four kids (Gabriella, 17; Adam, Jr., 15; Calique, 13; and Charles, 9) along with Maggie's younger sister Susie.

Here are four favorite recipes that continue to please my customers.

Magnolia Chili

MAKES: 8 servings

PREP. TIME: 15 minutes

COOKING TIME: 40 minutes

INGREDIENTS:

- 1 garlic clove, chopped finely
- ½ half green pepper, chopped finely
- ½ medium onion, chopped finely
- 2 lbs. stuffed magnolia or Italian sausage, chopped
- ½ cup chili powder
- 2 Tbsp. Worcestershire sauce
- 2–16 oz. cans diced tomatoes
- 2–16 oz. cans tomato sauce
- 8 oz. can whole kernel corn, undrained
- 2 cups water

1. Sauté garlic, green pepper, and onion with sausage over medium high heat in cooking pot for about five minutes. Stir in all remaining ingredients.

2. Simmer on medium heat for at least 30 minutes before serving. *The longer the simmer the more flavorful the stew.*

Smoky Mountain Fried Corn

MAKES: 4 servings

PREP. TIME: 10 minutes

COOKING TIME: 30 minutes

INGREDIENTS:

- 8 oz. lean bacon
- 16-oz. can whole kernel corn, drained
- 16-oz. can cream corn
- ¼ cup brown sugar
- ¼ cup apple cider vinegar
- ½ green pepper, chopped finely

1. In large skillet over medium high heat fry bacon until crisp. Remove bacon strips from skillet and chop.

2. Stir both cans of corn into skillet, dissolve brown sugar in corn, stir in vinegar, and add chopped bacon and green pepper. Simmer on medium heat for 20 minutes. Serve warm as a side.

Pineapple Asian Chicken

MAKES: 8 servings

PREP. TIME: 15 minutes

COOKING TIME: 45 minutes

INGREDIENTS:

2 lbs. chicken pieces of cook's choice

4 Tbsp. onion, chopped finely

4 Tbsp. fresh garlic, chopped finely

4 Tbsp. fresh ginger, chopped finely

18-oz. can tomato sauce

8 oz. can crushed pineapple

1. On well-greased baking sheet, roast chicken in 375° oven until fully cooked (30–40 minutes).

2. Meanwhile, in large pot mix onion, garlic, and ginger with tomato sauce and pineapple. Simmer sauce for 20 minutes. Pour over cooked chicken and broil for 5 minutes. Serve.

Caramel Apple Crisp

MAKES: 8 servings

PREP. TIME: 15 minutes

COOKING TIME: 30 minutes

INGREDIENTS:

8 Granny Smith apples, peeled and sliced

8 oz. butter (2 sticks) divided

½ cup flour

2 cups sugar

2 Tbsp. vanilla extract

8 oz. can sweetened condensed milk

1 cup brown sugar

1. Arrange apples in 9″ x 13″ pan.

2. In large bowl, melt one stick butter in microwave. Stir in flour, sugar, and vanilla extract. Mix with fork and spread mixture over apples. Bake at 350° for 35 minutes.

3. While baking, make the caramel sauce. In large skillet over medium heat melt remaining stick of butter; add condensed milk and brown sugar. Whisk fast until mixture thickens.

4. Remove baked apple crisp from oven. Pour caramel over top, set for 10 minutes, then serve with vanilla ice cream.

David Wenger

David Wenger, *Co-director*
Hermitage Retreat Center, Three Rivers, Michigan

Learn to trust your culinary intuition.

One Sunday afternoon when I was around sixteen, I had the urge to make a pie. Maybe it was having a summer afternoon at home alone, with no one to question what I was doing or to tell me how to do it. Though I had never made a pie, the process wasn't foreign because I had often watched my mother make pies. I followed a recipe for the crust and fresh strawberry filling. It was quite simple. I hope I topped it with whipped cream. When my mother came home we had a piece of pie together. She still reminds me of my first culinary adventure.

The rhythm of creating sustenance for the body has been a continuous practice for me over three decades. It began as a newly married man when Naomi and I made dinner together after each coming home from work. By the time we had children I was equally adept at making dinner as Naomi.

For years when the children were growing up we had "Pizza Fridays" which didn't involve calling the local pizza parlor for a delivery. We made the dough and sauce from scratch. With three pizza pans, we each got to top one half of a pizza to our own liking. The challenge was identifying the dividing line after baking.

On our first daughter's fifteenth birthday I wanted to bless her by making her favorite breakfast (pancakes) before she left for school. Even though it meant getting up extra early, it turned out to be a blessing given and received. Since then I have been making my family breakfast each school day. Oatmeal pancakes are a family favorite, especially with orange or berry sauce.

I started baking bread on a regular basis because I couldn't decide which bread to buy at the grocery store. I didn't want any of the bread offered there. One day I skipped the bread aisle and went home and made bread. This was a much more satisfying way to come by our daily bread. I created space in my daily rhythm to include making bread every two or three days, enough to supply my family and guests.

Most of my cooking now is done in the home-like kitchen of The Hermitage in rural southern Michigan, a contemplative retreat center and place of welcoming hospitality for guests who come to retreat into solitude and silence.

I credit my mother Mary and my wife Naomi as my mentors in the kitchen. Mom depends mostly on recipes. Naomi reads cookbooks, but rarely follows a recipe. I rely on recipes most often but I do trust my own intuition at times— particularly when it comes to using leftovers creatively.

Oatmeal Pancakes with Orange Sauce

MAKES: 6 servings

PREP. TIME: 15 minutes

COOKING TIME: 15 minutes

INGREDIENTS:

1 ½ cups quick oats

2 cups milk

1 cup flour

2 ½ tsp. baking powder

1 tsp. salt

2 eggs, beaten

¼ cup wheat germ

⅓ cup vegetable oil

1. Pour milk over oats; cover and let stand for 5 minutes.
2. Sift together flour, baking powder, and salt.
3. Stir beaten eggs into oat mixture; add sifted dry ingredients and wheat germ. Stir in oil.
4. Bake on 375° griddle until golden brown, turning only once when tops are covered with bubbles.

SAUCE

1 cup sugar

2 Tbsp. cornstarch

2 cups orange juice

2 Tbsp. lemon juice

¼ cup butter

1. Mix sugar and cornstarch in a saucepan. Stir in juices.
2. Cook over medium heat until mixture is thick and clear. Boil for 1 minute, stirring constantly.
3. Remove from heat and blend in butter.
4. Serve warm over pancakes.

Rustic No-Knead Bread

MAKES: 2 round loaves

PREP. TIME: 45 minutes

RESTING: 12 + 2 hours

BAKING TIME: 35 minutes

INGREDIENTS:

2 ½ cups whole-wheat flour

3 ½ cups all-purpose flour

½ (scant) tsp. instant yeast

2 ½ tsp. salt

3 ¼ cups water

1. In a large bowl combine flours, yeast, and salt. Add the water, and stir until blended; dough will be shaggy and sticky. Cover bowl with plastic wrap. Let dough rest at least 12 hours, preferably 18, at 70° room temperature.

2. Dough is ready when surface is dotted with bubbles. Using a firm spatula or flexible dough scraper, release dough from the sides of the bowl, scraping it down and folding it over on itself several times.

3. Prepare two pie pans by lining with a cotton cloth (cut up t-shirts work well), leaving enough hanging over one side to cover the dough once in the pan. Generously coat cloth with flour (rice flour works best at keeping dough from sticking to cloth).

4. Place bowl of water near dough bowl so you can keep hands wet while handling dough. (Sticky dough does not stick to wet hands). Divide dough in half. Make hands wet and lift half the dough out of bowl. Gently and quickly shape dough into a ball (if dough sticks to your hands get them wet again). Place dough onto cotton-lined pie pan. Sprinkle flour (rice or wheat) on top of round loaf. Cover with remaining half of cotton cloth. Repeat procedure for second loaf. Let dough rise about 1 ¼ hours.

5. At least 30 minutes before dough is ready, heat oven to 450°. Put two 3-quart heavy covered pots (cast iron, enamel, Pyrex, or ceramic) in the oven as it heats.

6. When dough is ready, remove a pot from the oven one at a time, uncover dough and carefully lift sides of cloth so that dough is held as if in a hammock; gently turn dough over into hot pot. (As you practice this move you may eventually be able to land the dough into the pan's center, but until then, don't worry if it looks like a mess, just shake the pan once or twice to distribute dough more evenly and it will straighten out as it bakes.) Cover with lid and bake 20 minutes, remove lid, and bake another 15 minutes, until loaves are beautifully browned. Cool on rack. (The bread will slice best when it is completely cooled.)

Honey Whole-Wheat Bread

MAKES: 2 loaves

PREP. TIME: 45 minutes

RESTING: 2 ½ hours

BAKING TIME: 45 minutes

INGREDIENTS:

3 cups whole-wheat flour

1 Tbsp. yeast

3 cups hot water

½ cup honey

2 Tbsp. oil

1 Tbsp. salt

1 cup additional whole-wheat flour

4–4 ½ cups all-purpose flour

1. In a large bowl combine 3 cups whole-wheat flour and yeast.

2. Stir together hot water, honey, and oil until dissolved. (To eliminate the sticky mess of measuring honey separately, use a 4-cup measure, filling with hot water to the 3-cup line and adding honey to 3 ½-cup line.)

3. Pour liquid over flour mixture and stir well for 3 minutes. Stir in salt and remaining flours. (Incorporating flour into dough requires patience; add about ½ cup flour at a time, mixing into the dough before adding more.) When dough begins to pull away from sides of bowl (usually with 1–1 ½ cups of flour remaining), turn onto a lightly floured work surface and knead for 8–10 minutes, gradually incorporating remaining flour as needed to prevent sticking. Dough should feel soft and smooth.

4. Place dough in large, lightly oiled bowl. Roll dough around bowl to coat with oil. Cover bowl tightly (plastic wrap works well) and let rise until double in bulk (around 1–1 ½ hours).

5. After first rise, punch down dough and knead for 1–2 minutes. Divide dough in half and briefly knead each half, forming dough into shape of a bread pan. Place dough into a lightly greased pan and cover pans with a towel. Let rise 40–45 minutes, or until doubled.

6. Bake at 375° for 35–45 minutes. (Bread that registers 190° on an instant read thermometer is done.) Turn out of pans onto drying rack to cool.

Black Bean and Sweet Potato Stew

MAKES: 4 servings (can be doubled, tripled, or quadrupled)

PREP. TIME: 15 minutes

COOKING TIME: 30 minutes

INGREDIENTS:

3 Tbsp. olive oil

1 cup coarsely chopped onion

1 green pepper, seeded and coarsely chopped

2 cloves garlic, finely chopped

¼ - ½ jalapeño pepper finely chopped (optional)

1 Tbsp. chili powder

2 cups diced, peeled sweet potato

2 cups diced tomatoes

2 cups cooked black beans

3 Tbs. chopped cilantro

Salt

Freshly ground black pepper

1. In a large saucepan heat the olive oil. Add the onion, green pepper, garlic, and jalapeño pepper and cook over medium heat until the vegetables begin to soften, about 4 minutes. Stir in the chili powder and cook for 1 minute. Add sweet potato and enough water (about 1 cup) to barely cover them. Cover and cook, stirring occasionally, until potato can just be pierced with a sharp knife, about 10 minutes.

2. Add tomatoes and beans. Simmer stew, uncovered over medium-low heat until potato is very tender, about 8 minutes. To thicken stew slightly mash about a quarter of the beans against side of the pan.

3. Stir in cilantro and season with salt and pepper to taste.

John Bender

John Bender, *Writer-Editor* (actively retired)
Elkhart, Indiana

Food was fun while I was growing up.

Mother was my main cooking mentor, along with grandmothers and aunts—especially Aunt Elvera. Not only did Vera cook among the best, she knew how to enthrall us youngsters with a picnic in the woods.

My mother told stories of growing up baking bread, churning butter, making maple syrup, canning, raising chickens, butchering, gardening, and tending an orchard.

Paternal grandfather Solomon, "Pop," did custom butchering. In two smokehouses he cured sausages and hams. Pop and Grandma Rachel took dressed chickens, eggs, and garden produce to the Kitchener (Ontario, Canada) Farmers' Market. What a thrill, in the wee hours of Saturday morning, to travel with them in their 1937 Chevrolet the seventeen miles to market. Bushels of peaches, pears, and apples sometimes came home for canning. Canning season from our farm garden included corn, pickles, tomatoes, and beans. We made apple butter by the crock-full.

One of my earliest memories of actual cooking involved stirring the porridge, our almost daily breakfast staple. Since the kitchen was the "professional" domain of females, the "hunters and gatherers" in the extended family found little recourse in actually preparing a meal. We could fry eggs, boil potatoes, open a jar of canned sausage, make popcorn, wash dishes, and so on, but meal planning and cooking lodged with the distaff. The men, though, cranked homemade ice cream for family gatherings.

For our high school graduating class at Rockway Mennonite School, the guys cooked an outdoor breakfast. I remember frying dozens of duck eggs, scrambled, in bacon fat. During a year as an exchange visitor in Germany, among other duties, I tended a two-acre garden at a church center near

Karlsruhe. I had the pleasure of "manning" the wooden pounder to stamp shredded cabbage for sauerkraut.

In 1975, I took a seven-week cooking class with Arletta Lovejoy, then the proprietor of the Patchwork Quilt Country Inn, near Middlebury, Indiana. It was fun, helpful, and on "graduation night" we got to eat what we as a class prepared that evening.

I'm not fussy about food. Comfort food suits me fine, as do more exotic tastes and preparation methods. I've enjoyed collecting and reading cookbooks, although in 2012, I gave a bunch away for a local fund-raiser.

My style of cooking has been less following detailed recipes and more mixing and matching, such as making creative use of leftovers. I do appreciate and follow recipes, yet give me 30 minutes, a fridge with leftovers, spice and pantry shelves, a fry pan, a blender, and a toaster, and I'm in meal-time-happy-prep mode. My wife Marty and friends have paid tribute to the surprisingly successful results—most of the time.

Most of all, through my experiences in cooking I have gained a new appreciation for all the cooks in my life, past and present. They have and continue to provide fine food for body, mind and spirit. I am happy to do my part against the distinguished backdrop of all the delightful tastes and people around the table—and picnic blanket.

Quick Bites

MAKES: 8 servings

PREP. TIME: 5 minutes

INGREDIENTS:

1 cup pitted prunes

1 cup large green olives

1. Press an olive on top of a pitted prune. Presto, you have a finger food appetizer.

2. For each prune, or if you prefer to call it a dried plum, top with a medium or large size green olive for a combined sweet and salty taste. You also can use an almond stuffed olive, a small piece of spicy cheese such as pepper jack, or flavored cream cheese. Serve at room temperature. Easy, tasty, even a conversation item.

Veggie Crunch

MAKES: 4 servings

PREP. TIME: 10 minutes

COOKING TIME: 5 minutes

INGREDIENTS:

6 medium carrots, cut in half and sliced lengthwise, then cut crosswise for 2-inch sticks

½ green bell pepper, chopped in small bits

2 Tbsp. olive oil

¼ tsp. salt

SAUCE

1 Tbsp. orange marmalade

¼ cup rice vinegar

1. In a hot skillet heat oil. Add vegetables and cook for 3 minutes, turning once.

2. Toss in a serving dish with salt.

3. Mix marmalade and vinegar; spoon sauce on vegetables.

Poached Salmon

MAKES: 4 servings

PREP. TIME: 10 minutes

COOKING TIME: 10 minutes

INGREDIENTS:

1 pound salmon fillets

½ cup salt

12 cups water

1. Dissolve salt in water and bring to rapid boil. Turn heat down to a simmer (do not boil), immerse the salmon, and cover for 8 minutes.

2. Remove salmon to serving platter, allowing it to finish on the platter. (This cooking method does not add saltiness to the fish, but rather preserves the succulent juices.) Serve warm or cold, plain or dress with sauce or condiment of choice. Serve with boiled potatoes and fresh vegetables.

Easter Lilies

MAKES: 24 cookies

PREP. TIME: 15 minutes

BAKING TIME: 10 minutes

For each of us six children, my mother Leona hand-wrote a number of recipes of her own, commenting: "I have found these recipes helpful through the years and some handed down from my mother." This is a long-standing family recipe that "blooms" once a year for Easter dessert.

INGREDIENTS:

2 eggs, beaten

½ cup white sugar

Dash of salt

½ cup all-purpose flour

2 tsp. baking powder

1. Mix beaten eggs with dry ingredients. Drop teaspoonfuls on greased cookie sheet.

2. Bake about 10 minutes in 350° oven. Do not over bake.

3. Take off sheet with spatula as soon as baked and pinch one end together to shape like a lily leaf.

4. Cool, then fill with scoop of ice cream and enjoy.

Christmas Turnip

MAKES: 8 servings

PREP. TIME: 20 minutes

BAKING TIME: 1 hour

The turnip has been a traditional vegetable dish for some family gatherings at Christmas, and at other times too during its peak season from October through March. It can be made ahead of time and reheated in the microwave or oven.

INGREDIENTS:

4 medium turnips, peeled and cut in ¾-inch cubes

1 medium onion, diced

1 potato, peeled and cut in ¾-inch cubes

4 cups water

2 large apples (Cortland, Granny Smith, or Spy), cored and sliced thinly

2 Tbsp. butter, softened

¼ tsp. cinnamon

TOPPING

⅓ cup brown sugar

⅓ cup all-purpose flour

2 Tbsp. butter

1. In saucepan, uncovered, over medium heat cook turnips, onion, and potato in water until just crunchy soft.

2. Mix apples with butter and cinnamon. In large casserole, alternate layers of vegetables and apple slices.

3. Mix together topping ingredients to form crumbs and sprinkle on top layer in casserole.

4. Bake at 300° about an hour. Serve warm.

A few quotes from Mother Leona's recipe files:

God gives us the ingredients for our daily bread, but he expects us to do the baking.

Many are called, but few get up for breakfast.

Congratulate yourself on each small improvement, whether in the kitchen, school, or on the job.

Remember the steam kettle. Although up to its neck in hot water, it continues to sing.

Marshall King

Marshall King, *Community Editor*
The Elkhart Truth, Elkhart, Indiana

Writing about food is a joy.

I'm just a guy who likes to eat.

As a young newspaper reporter, I'd spend much of my mornings wondering and talking with a coworker about what I'd have for lunch. When the time came for the newspaper to add a restaurant column, the managing editor tapped me. That led to meals out, and eventually becoming a critic.

I'm still just a guy who likes to eat, but after more than twelve years of writing about food professionally, people rely on me to give them good information about restaurants and the dishes they serve.

As a child, I loved my mother's Amish-Mennonite-style cooking. As a college student, I first read Laurie Colwin's *Home Cooking* and *More Home Cooking,* and thought, "Somebody can do that? You can really write about food?"

Aside from writing about food for *The Elkhart Truth* and www.eTruth.com, I'm the managing editor. We're busy gathering, posting, and publishing news on Elkhart County, Indiana. But at least three times a day, I have to eat. And getting to write about it is a joy.

Deep-Fried Turkey

By this time, deep-fried turkey isn't novel. It got trendy. Lots of men have tried it. Lots of people have tasted a fried giant bird. But lots of people still say, "Isn't it dangerous?" That's kind of the point. Making a turkey in an oven isn't daring. Most of the time, it's not even tasty. And contributing to a summertime or fall event with a giant golden bird is appreciated.

EQUIPMENT:

An outdoor level space sheltered from the wind, preferably with an overhang in case it rains (safely away from the house and flammable objects)

Frying rig consisting of:

1 large pot (I prefer the 40-quart pot I got nearly two decades ago, but a smaller one uses less oil.)

An LP burner with LP tank

Long thermometer for the oil

Stand and hook that often come with turkey frying kits for lowering the turkey into the fryer, *or* metal colander fashioned with unfolded wire coat hooks

1 large stockpot or plastic bucket for brining the turkey (which container depends on refrigerator space or wherever you're cold-storing the bird overnight)

Newspapers

Welding gloves

INGREDIENTS:

35 lbs./5 gal. peanut oil or peanut oil blend

12-lb. turkey, thawed

Ice water

Cajun seasoning

BRINE:

1 gallon water *or* stock

1 Tbsp. peppercorns

2 Tbsp. Cajun seasoning

1 16-oz. bottle amber or dark beer

2 cups kosher salt (type of salt matters because of crystal size)

½ cup brown sugar

> **Tip:** The bird may be dark in spots and not look like its pale, pasty cousins that emerge from the oven; it'll taste better though.

The night before you fry:

1. Lower the thawed bird, even still in the packaging, into the pot and cover the bird with water.
2. Remove the bird and mark the level of the water. That's how much oil you need to put in the pot after you wash the raw turkey drippings out of it.
3. To make the brine, combine ingredients in stock pot and bring to boil. Cool.
4. Unwrap bird; remove giblets, neck, and timer (if any).
5. Place in plastic bucket or stockpot, pour brine over bird, and add ice water to cover, weighting bird down if needed. Keep cold, either in refrigerator or a garage (if the temperature is 40° or below).

The day you fry:

1. Light burner under pot and heat oil to 375°.
2. Remove turkey from brine. Rinse and pat dry. Spread newspaper on the counter and liberally coat the bird, inside and out, with Cajun seasoning.

To fry:

1. Place turkey in colander or on frying kit stand. When oil reaches temperature, don welding gloves and lower bird gently into oil. If there's ice still in the bird, it'll hiss and pop more than you may want. And if you filled the pot too full of oil, it'll overflow. Whatever you do, don't drop the bird into the hot oil.
2. Cover pot partially if you have a lid, but don't cover completely—steam from the frying bird needs to escape.
3. Fry an estimated 3 ½ minutes per pound. At the end of that time, raise bird from oil and use an instant-read meat thermometer to test the temperature. If the leg joint and breast are 155°, remove bird from oil. If not, lower and cook several minutes and check again. The bird will continue to cook and internal temperature will rise about 10 degrees after removed from oil.
4. Cool bird on newspaper. Once the turkey cools enough, you can serve whole or carve it with a knife, fork, and your hands (use latex or plastic gloves if you have them.) The heat makes the bones more brittle and it's not hard to break the turkey down once it cools. You can also save the bones to make stock.

Ribeye Steaks with Sweet-Salty Butter

Beef is good. Ribeyes are one of the best cuts because of the flavor from the fat in the meat. Adding a bit of butter, sweetness and bacon doesn't hurt. Just don't eat it every night.

INGREDIENTS:

5 slices quality bacon, fried crisp

1 stick (½ cup) butter, room temperature

¼ cup light molasses or sorghum

1 Tbsp. bourbon, optional

Plastic wrap

Coarse salt, preferably kosher

Pepper, freshly cracked

4 beef ribeye steaks, cut 1- to 1 ½-inch thick

To make sweet-salty butter

Cut cooled fried bacon in small pieces, mix with softened butter, molasses, (and bourbon if desired) in small bowl until smooth. Spoon onto plastic wrap and form into a small log. Refrigerate until firm.

To prepare steaks

1. Remove from refrigerator; coat both sides with thin layer of salt and pepper, and let warm on kitchen counter at least 30 minutes.
2. Prepare charcoal fire until a light coating of ash is on the charcoal, or preheat gas grill.
3. Grill steaks over hot flame to sear outside and allow at least four minutes on a side to get to medium.
4. To check doneness, use a thermometer, the peek-and-check method, or test firmness. A looser steak is less done. A firmer steak is more done.
5. To have a medium-rare steak, remove when internal temperature is 130˚.
6. Allow meat to rest at least 10 minutes after removing from grill. If you cut into a steak too soon, it'll lose more juice than desired.
7. Top steaks with medallions of sliced butter and serve.

DIY Vanilla

INGREDIENTS:

10 or more vanilla beans, either Madagascar or Bourbon variety (or both)

1 bottle vodka (or other spirits such as whiskey, bourbon or rum)

1. Slice each bean lengthwise and place in a quart canning jar.
2. Cover with alcohol.
3. Allow to sit in a dark, cool place for at least two months and preferably longer. Ten beans are enough for a quart if you have enough time, but if you're short on time, use more beans. When the concoction smells like the real vanilla, it's ready.
4. Using a funnel, fill small bottles and label for use. You can also ask your friends to bring you jars to fill. Cut a small portion of a vanilla bean to put in each bottle.

You can use any jar and cover the beans with alcohol. You can put the beans into the liquor bottle itself after removing a few ounces, but getting beans in and out of a small-necked jar is difficult.

To get beans, don't pay $5 each at a specialty shop. You can buy a bunch online for much less money. You may even be able to pay about a dollar or less depending on how many you buy. For instance, eBay has great deals on vanilla beans from reliable vendors.

You can buy vanilla, but when you make your own, you also create a great holiday gift. This do-it-yourself recipe is easy to make and impresses friends or loved ones. All you need is vanilla beans, alcohol, and plenty of advance time.

Mango Salsa

INGREDIENTS:

2 ripe mangos, peeled and seeded

½ fresh pineapple

2 oranges, one juiced and one peeled

1 red bell pepper, seeded

1 green bell pepper, seeded

1 jalapeño pepper, seeded without inner membrane

¼ cup honey

½ cup apple cider vinegar, or rice wine vinegar

1. Dice all mangos, pineapple, orange, and peppers into ⅜-inch chunks, except the jalapeño which should be diced smaller. For hotter salsa, add more jalapeño.

2. Combine in serving bowl with honey and vinegar. Serve with chips, fish, or chicken.

When my wife Bethany and I travel to visit family in Florida, we have a tradition of buying fresh fish, making mango salsa, and serving them together. The produce markets of Florida in January make this easy to make, but it can be made in other places at other times too. If you like something more or have less of something, it's not a major issue. The key is to feature the fruit and allow the juices to blend with a little acid and peppers.

Stanley Kropf

Stanley Kropf, *Businessman* (actively retired)
Port Townsend, Washington

Be free to depart from tradition.

I grew up in the cradle of an Amish Mennonite community where Sunday dinner was the social center of our week. Gathering after worship in each other's homes, we followed the same routine every week: the children played together before and after dinner; the women cooked dinner and washed the dishes; and the men sat around talking and napping. On one particular Sunday afternoon our extended family gathered at my Uncle Earl and Aunt Elsie's home. The men were sitting in the living room doing their Sunday pre-dinner gabbing—that is, all except Uncle Earl. He was in the kitchen with the women—cooking. Such freedom to depart from a traditional role planted a seed that encouraged me to do the same. This vivid childhood memory marks the beginning of my journey into the kitchen.

Skip ahead a decade plus several years to my early marriage. For a very practical reason I began cooking breakfast in the morning: my wife Marlene needed to leave early to drive to the high school where she taught, and I needed only to walk a block to my work. It simply made sense for me to prepare breakfast. Having just moved to Portland, Oregon from a rural community, we brought along the farm breakfast menu of fried eggs and bacon, toast, and coffee (and on special occasions, pancakes or waffles). Since Marlene's work over the years has usually demanded more time than mine, I gradually assumed more and more of the cooking responsibilities. For the past decade I have been the primary cook in our family.

In 1983 we moved to Elkhart, Indiana where I was employed by the Mennonite Church. In that setting I had the wonderful privilege of participating in a men's cooking club. Willard Roth invited me to join a group of four men whose sole agenda was to take turns planning and preparing a meal for the sheer pleasure of cooking and eating. Our guests were our spouses. Because of a move, the club diminished to three men, and later just Willard and I remained. With only two of us left, we began inviting others to join in the meals we prepared. I do not recall duplicating one meal or even one dish over the two decades of our feasting together.

Over the years my cooking has been inspired by international travel or by eating in restaurants with ethnic specialties. When I return home I attempt to recreate the menus I've enjoyed, experimenting and adapting until I'm satisfied with the results.

Recently Marlene and I moved to Port Townsend, Washington, a small seaside town on the northeast corner of the Olympic Peninsula. As retired persons on a fixed income and being less active than before, we need less food, but our enjoyment of tasty food is not at all diminished. Small, tasty portions with a complementary glass of wine have become a focus of my cooking.

I offer a set of favorite tapa recipes to this collection—a perfect solution for a meal of small and tasty dishes, which, when one adds good conversation with friends, is a delightful way to spend an evening.

A meal of tapas has no one dish as the main dish. Rather, it is made up of a series of dishes with only enough food to serve the diners one or two small mouth-watering portions—always chased with a favorite beverage. Taste is, of course, important, but no more important than presentation. Some say that with tapas, "presentation is everything." In North America we might call tapas hors d'oeuvres or appetizers; in Britain, they'd be called starters.

When I serve tapas, I like to invite my guests to bring one tapa along for the table. I prepare several and provide beverages. There is no magic number of tapas to serve, and there is no set menu more appropriate than another. What is essential is time to eat at a leisurely pace. Each tapa is offered one at a time and often with a clean plate to enhance the presentation. A red or white sangria is a most agreeable beverage. Some people like sherry, but any wine will do.

Peppery Avocado on Grilled Bread

MAKES: 4 servings, 2 per person

PREP. TIME: 10 minutes (includes grilling)

INGREDIENTS:

8 thin slices of bread, sliced at a diagonal (I like whole grain or artisan bread), lightly grilled or toasted until crisp

1 ripe buttery avocado, sliced in ¼"-slices

Extra virgin (first cold pressed) olive oil for drizzling

Sea salt

Red pepper flakes

1. Rub each side of the grilled bread with garlic.

2. Arrange avocado slices on bread.

3. Drizzle with oil; sprinkle, to taste, with sea salt and crushed red pepper flakes

Devils on Horseback

MAKES: 4 servings, 2 or 3 per person

PREP. TIME: 10 minutes

BAKING TIME: 25 minutes

This delightful combination of dried plums, crunchy almonds, and bacon, topped with mango chutney, always disappears quickly when served.

INGREDIENTS:

- 8–12 pitted dried plums
- 8–12 whole almonds
- 4–6 bacon slices (½ slice to wrap around each plum)
- Wooden tooth picks
- Mango chutney
- Fresh parsley sprigs

1. Insert one almond into each dried plum (simulating the plum pit). Wrap each stuffed plum with ½ slice of bacon and pin together with a wooden tooth pick. Place on a baking sheet sprayed with vegetable oil.

2. Bake at 400° until bacon is cooked through (20–25 minutes).

3. Remove from oven, top with a dollop of mango chutney and garnish with parsley sprigs.

Garlic Whipped Potatoes with Prosciutto-Wrapped Asparagus

MAKES: 4 servings, 1 per person

PREP. TIME: 15 minutes

COOKING TIME: 20 minutes

INGREDIENTS:

2 medium new white
   potatoes, diced

1 quart water (twice)

2 garlic cloves, minced

Half & half (quantity varies
   according to how mushy
   one prefers potatoes)

2 Tbsp. butter

1 Tbsp. mayonnaise

½ tsp. salt

8 asparagus spears,
   fibrous ends removed

4 thin prosciutto slices

Paprika and fresh chopped
   chives for garnish

1. Put potatoes into kettle, cover with water, and cook with moderate heat until tender (about 20 minutes). Drain potatoes. Add garlic, and whip with electric beater, adding half & half until potatoes are cook's preferred consistency. Mix in butter, mayonnaise, and salt.

2. While potatoes are cooking prepare the prosciutto-wrapped asparagus spears. Place spears in boiling water and parboil for one minute. Remove and cool immediately under cold water. Wrap two spears with one slice of prosciutto. Refrigerate until served.

3. Place ice cream-size-scoop of potatoes on four warmed plates. Garnish with chives and sprinkle with paprika. Set one of the prosciutto-wrapped asparagus bundles alongside potatoes. Serve immediately.

Roasted Red Pepper Crostini with Anchovy Filets

MAKES: 8 servings

PREP. TIME: 15 minutes + roasting

MARINATING: 8 hours

INGREDIENTS:

- 1 red pepper, to be roasted (or a jar of roasted red peppers)
- 2 garlic cloves, coarsely chopped
- ¼ tsp. salt
- olive oil, to cover red pepper slices (reserve as marinade)
- 1 baguette, sliced diagonally into thin rounds and grilled or toasted
- 2 oz. Parmesan cheese, shaved into very thin slices
- 1 jar anchovy filets
- 1 Tbsp. fresh parsley, chopped

1. Place whole red pepper under broiler, turning periodically until the skin blackens. Cool, then peel skin, and slice pepper into ¾-inch strips.

2. Combine roasted red pepper slices, chopped garlic, and salt in small dish. Cover with olive oil. Set aside to marinate for at least 8 hours.

3. Cover each toasted bread slice with roasted red pepper slices; place a strip or two of shaved cheese on each slice. Spoon a small amount of olive oil marinade over each bread slice; sprinkle with chopped parsley, and serve with anchovy filets on the side.

Traditional Shrimp Tapas

MAKES: 4 servings, 3 shrimp per person

PREP. TIME: 10 minutes

COOKING TIME: 10 minutes

INGREDIENTS:

3 oz. virgin olive oil

2 cloves garlic, finely minced

1 tsp. red pepper flakes

12 large fresh shrimp, peeled

Juice of 1 fresh lemon or lime

2–3 oz. cognac (may substitute sherry, brandy, or vermouth; each different spirit will alter the taste)

1 tsp. sweet paprika

3 tsp. fresh parsley, chopped

1. Heat oil in skillet on medium heat; sauté the garlic and red pepper flakes for about one minute until the garlic turns brown (take care not to burn garlic).

2. Increase heat to high and immediately add shrimp, lemon juice, cognac, and paprika. Stir to coat the shrimp and continue to stir briskly. Sauté until the shrimp turns pink and begins to curl (about 3 minutes).

3. Remove shrimp to a warm dish or serve from the pan. Season with salt and pepper to taste, sprinkle with chopped parsley. Serve with bread.

French Peasant Bouillabaisse

MAKES: 6 servings

PREP. TIME: 20 minutes

COOKING TIME: 40 minutes

INGREDIENTS:

- ¾ cup olive oil
- 2 onions, sliced
- 2 leeks, sliced (include about 2 inches of green top)
- 2 celery stalks, sliced
- 1 green bell pepper, chopped
- 1 clove garlic, chopped finely
- ½ cup parsley, chopped
- 1 tsp. paprika
- 1 Tbsp. dried thyme
- 1 tsp. saffron
- ½ tsp. cayenne
- 6 scallops
- 1 crab, cracked
- 1 small lobster, cut
- 2 lbs. hardshell clams
- 1 lb. mussels
- 6 prawns
- 1 lb. red snapper
- 1 lb. halibut
- 28-oz. can stewed tomatoes
- 2 cups chicken broth
- 1 cup sweet white wine

1. Heat oil in skillet on medium heat. Saute onions, leeks, celery stalks, and bell pepper until golden brown. Stir in garlic and parsley and saute 1 more minute.

2. Add paprika, thyme, saffron, and cayenne, seafood, tomatoes, and broth. Simmer gently for 30 minutes.

3. Add wine just before serving.

Serving Tip: I like to serve this in a pot or deep casserole for a rustic look.

Tip: You can substitute other non-fresh water fish as you choose.

Willard Swartley

Willard Swartley, *Professor Emeritus*
Anabaptist Mennonite Biblical Seminary, Elkhart, Indiana

Kitchen diversion qualifies as Sabbath rest.

My journey into cooking or jamming! It began when I was visiting my wife Mary's sister in Germany in 1975. With free time and tasty apples at hand, I happened upon a Roman Apple cake recipe. I thought, why not try it? (I no longer have that recipe, but numerous variations are readily available.) The cake turned out to be quite tasty, and prompted me to say "I can do this too."

Stage two came when Mary's dad, John E. Lapp, informed us that mulberries (we had a big tree) and sour cherries (we had a smaller tree) go well together, making the most delicious pies. Mary baked a pie, and it was delicious. I later made a jam (recipe follows). I began to think that what grows together (in various seasons) goes together. So I began experimenting with blackberry, peach, and most recently adding rhubarb and even cantaloupe to jam recipes.

I spend most of my time writing, reading, and editing. I often seek something different to do. Because of heart-health limitations, I've found that cooking and baking provides the right diversion. Kitchen activity, however, does not replace regular morning exercises; baking cookies or crisps or making jam is the diversion I need. It yields an immediate reward and provides tasty food to enjoy. It makes me feel fulfilled, and at times even qualifies for Sabbath rest from other labors.

Marva Dawn identifies four dimensions of Sabbath-keeping crucial to faithful Jewish and Christian living—each with ethical import: *Ceasing*, to deepen our repentance from self-planning our future; *Resting*, to strengthen faith, breathing God's grace; *Embracing*, to apply faith practically to our values and friendships; and *Feasting*, to celebrate the joy of God's love and the Sabbath's foretaste of the age to come. Sabbath renews work, home, economics, education, environment, writing, and worship. Sabbath-keeping is essential for shalom-wholeness. Each of these aspects is, in part, present when I cease from my usual work and spend time baking, with aromas that remind me of God's creation and renew my spirit.

One of my students gave me some "Sabbath-wear"—bowls and serving plate that fit the occasion of beauty that "breathe God's grace." Often what I bake I share with others. A loaf of banana bread may be split in three parts, with one part going to one of my friends. What I bake fits feasting, and this is best experienced when I can share cake, crisps, or cookies with friends. If I worked in the kitchen most of the time, six days a week, my baking would not qualify as Sabbath renewal. One thing sure, I do not bake with the computer. It rests on the Sabbath, which for me is important, and one discipline I seek to keep at least until Sunday celebrations are over. I may late in the evening check for email from friends or children, but that is the exception.

My joy is to experiment with what God enables to grow in a particular season. I love to experiment (no catastrophes to date). Along with the fruit spread recipes which follow, a baking standby for all seasons is a simple, quick cookie recipe.

Kumquat Marmalade

MAKES: 3 to 5 jars depending on size

PREP. TIME: 30 minutes

SOAKING TIME: 30 minutes

COOKING TIME: 30 minutes

I discovered kumquats when visiting Florida in-laws and adapted a citrus recipe to come up with this unique bread topping. But I warn you, this is a labor-intensive project.

INGREDIENTS:

3 cups kumquats

1 qt. water (room temperature)

1 tsp. baking soda

3 cups water

1 lemon, squeezed for juice

1 pkg. Sure Jell

3 cups sugar

1. Wash kumquats and soak for 30 minutes in 1 quart of water with baking soda.

2. Cut soaked kumquats in half, and grind after removing seeds.

3. In heavy saucepan, boil the combined fruit, 3 cups of water, and lemon juice, and then follow instructions on Sure Jell package. Once it comes to boil, stir in sugar and bring to full boil again for 1 minute. Remove from burner and pour into warmed jam jars.

Mulberry-Cherry Jam

MAKES: 3 to 5 jars depending on size

PREP TIME: 15 minutes

COOKING TIME: varies

This is my most-liked jam. "What grows together goes together." This combination also makes a delicious fruit crisp.

INGREDIENTS:

3 cups mulberries, washed

2 ½ cups sour cherries

4 ½ cups sugar

1 pkg. Sure Jell

Follow instructions on Sure Jell package (you may reduce sugar without affecting outcome)

Blackberry-Rhubarb-Cantaloupe Jam

MAKES: 3 to 5 jars depending on size

PREP. TIME: 15 minutes

COOKING TIME: varies

My most recently discovered "goodie." Again, what grows together goes together. Earlier, I made only blackberry/peach jam, also (quite tasty). For this combination, use equal amounts of both fruits, with a bit less sugar, since peaches are usually sweet.

INGREDIENTS:

3 cups blackberries, juiced (put in blender, strain, use juice only)

2 cups rhubarb (put in blender, or cut into small pieces)

1 ½ cups cantaloupe (blend until juiced)

1 pkg. Sure Jell

Follow instructions on Sure Jell package (reduce sugar by ½ cup).

Crispy Oatmeal Raisin Cookies

MAKES: 40 cookies

PREP. TIME: 15 minutes

BAKING TIME: 10 minutes per sheet

This is my favorite cookie and since I vary the cereal and the dried fruit and yogurt, they taste different each time I bake. Many friends have asked me for the recipe; I share it here for those who want a cookie that is both healthy and tasty!

INGREDIENTS:

¾ cup brown sugar, packed

2 ½ to 3 Tbsp. margarine

4 oz. yogurt (any flavor works)

1 tsp. vanilla

1 egg + 1 egg white (or 1 Tbsp. liquid egg white)

3 cups cereal (choose from oatmeal raisin, quick oats, low-fat granola, rice crisps, or bran with raisins)

9 dried apricots, cut into small pieces (kiwi is good also)

¼ cup raisins or dried cranberries (or mix)

1 ¼ cups all-purpose flour

1 tsp. baking powder

½ tsp. salt, *optional*

½ tsp. cinnamon

1. Mix brown sugar, margarine, yogurt, vanilla, and egg in large bowl.
2. Stir in remaining ingredients. (If mixture is too dry, add a tablespoon or two of orange juice until dough is moist and a bit pasty.)
3. Drop by rounded teaspoonfuls about ½ inch apart on ungreased cookie sheet.
4. Bake in 400° oven until light brown, 8–10 minutes. Remove from oven and cool before storing.

Nephews

As word spread that Uncle Willard was working on a cross-generational cookbook with a masculine twist, several nephews (with a bit of prodding) sent along their stories and favorite recipes.

Gary Brunk (60-something)
Lawrence, Kansas

Seared Scallops and Egg Noodles

MAKES: 2 servings

PREP. TIME: 15 minutes

COOKING TIME: 30 minutes

INGREDIENTS:

⅔ to ¾ pounds dry sea scallops

8 oz. egg noodles or fettuccini

2 Tbsp. unsalted butter, divided

1 Tbsp. olive oil

Kosher salt and freshly ground black pepper

½ cup dry white wine, such as a sauvignon blanc

> **Tip:** To serve four, double ingredients, but avoid toughness by cooking scallops in two batches.

1. Remove small side muscle from scallops, rinse with cold water, pat dry. Slice each scallop to end up with two rounds per scallop; spread on a baking pan covered with absorbent towel.

2. Bring to boil 3–4 quarts water for cooking pasta. Based on cooking instructions, begin cooking noodles or fettuccine so that they can be drained a minute before you finish searing scallops (below). Pasta should be quite *al dente* when removed from the water. Meanwhile, warm two dinner plates.

3. Add 1 Tbsp. butter and the oil to a sauté pan on high heat. Pan needs to conduct heat evenly and be large enough to accommodate the scallop rounds without touching. Salt and pepper scallops. Once fat begins to smoke, gently add scallops; sear for one minute on each side. *Do not overcook or they will be tough.* Scallops should have a golden crust on each side while still being translucent in the center.

4. Remove scallops from pan, divide among two warmed dinner plates; cover so they remain warm. Turn heat under pan to highest setting, add wine. Reduce wine by one-half, add 1 Tbsp. butter and cooked pasta. Quickly toss pasta in wine and butter, add to plates with scallops and serve.

5. Serve with mixed lettuce tossed in a simple vinaigrette. A non-oaky dry white wine such as a sauvignon blanc nicely complements the food.

Jeff Metzler (40-something)
Minneapolis, Minnesota

My passion for cooking came to me late in my life. During the eighteen years that I spent working in the restaurant business, I was always impressed with the job that was done by the guys in the back. Night after night they would put out food that tasted as good as it looked. I would pick their brains for a new creation that later would end up as dinner for my soon-to-be wife. Cooking for me quickly became a form of relaxation. The kitchen is a sanctuary that allows me time to myself. I love taking a recipe and making it my own by creating new flavor profiles, or enhancing flavors that I already love. Here is a great refreshing starter that requires no direct heat to prepare.

Ceviche

PREP. TIME: 30 minutes

REFRIGERATION: 10 hours

INGREDIENTS:

1 ½ lbs red snapper fillets cut into ½-inch pieces

1 ½ lbs of raw shrimp, shelled and deveined, cut into ½-inch pieces

8 to 10 fresh limes

1 red onion, diced

1 ½ cup fresh tomato, seeded and chopped

1 green pepper, seeded and chopped

1 to 2 hot peppers, jalapeño or serrano, seeded and diced

2 tsp. sea salt

Dash of fresh ground pepper

Dash of oregano

Tabasco sauce to taste

Fresh cilantro

Avocado

Tortilla chips

1. Place snapper and shrimp in bowl. Halve limes and squeeze juice of each into bowl; there should be enough juice to cover seafood. Refrigerate covered up to 8 hours, stirring occasionally.
2. When snapper and shrimp have turned opaque, remove bowl and drain, leaving a little juice in bowl. Add onion, tomato, green pepper, hot pepper, seasonings, and fresh cilantro.
3. Place bowl back in fridge to allow mixture to cool and flavors to blend.
4. Serve with warmed tortilla chips and ripe slices of avocado.

Phil Metzler (50-something)
Columbus, Ohio

I learned to cook out of necessity when I was a junior in high school in Washington, D. C. My father was on extended assignment at the Mennonite Central Committee Peace Section and my mother was gone three days a week at graduate school. My options: cook or go hungry. Without a lot of direction and not much inclination to follow recipes, my modus operandi became "mix up whatever is in the fridge." I would chop and sauté every veggie in the house, create some sort of soy or tomato-based sauce and *voila*—dinner! Today, my family knows I can whip up something tasty even if there is "nothing" in the fridge.

In college I was guided by Doris Longacre's *More with Less* cookbook and started to expand my repertoire with Jeff Smith's *The Frugal Gourmet*. Here's a recipe that I make for my family, which they especially love.

Balsamic Brussels Sprouts

MAKES: 4 servings

PREP. TIME: 10 minutes

RESTING TIME: 25 minutes

INGREDIENTS:

1 lb. fresh Brussels sprouts

¼ cup water

¼ cup olive oil

¼ cup balsamic vinegar

kosher salt

coarsely ground black pepper

1. Clean the Brussels sprouts by cutting off the bottom of the stems and then peeling/pulling off the outer one or two layers of leaves. Slice the Brussels sprouts in half from top to bottom.

2. Put the sprouts in a microwavable bowl, add ¼ cup water and cover to seal. Microwave on High for about 3–4 minutes, just enough to steam and slightly soften them.

3. Heat a large flat-bottom skillet over high heat. Add enough olive oil to generously cover the bottom of the pan, about ¼ cup.

4. Drain the sprouts. When the oil is hot, add them to the skillet, arranging them as much as possible in a single layer, face (cut) side down.

5. Cook uncovered for 5–8 minutes without stirring. When the sprouts have a nice blackened crisp on their cut sides, stir and tumble them to sear their other sides as well.

6. After about 10 minutes, splash ¼ cup of balsamic vinegar onto the sprouts. Stir for another minute or two to evaporate a bit of the vinegar.

7. When they're as tender as you like them, season with a bit of salt and pepper and then serve them hot!

Todd Watson (40-something)
Dallas, Texas

My cooking journey: growing up I always watched my mom and grandma cook. I was entrusted to grill burgers, steaks, chops, and hot dogs—but that was the extent. It wasn't till I was out of college and on my own that I really started preparing food from scratch, moving on from the grill to more adventurous dishes. Once married I really started to cook, as my wife is an excellent cook and we enjoy working in the kitchen together. Now I enjoy preparing meats on the smoker, grilling, cooking fish of all shapes and styles, soups, pasta, and on and on. Here is a favorite that is unusual but great for calamari-lovers.

Brown Butter Pasta and Calamari

MAKES: 4 servings

PREP TIME: 20 minutes

COOKING TIME: 30 minutes

INGREDIENTS:

16 oz. farfalle pasta (Italian for butterfly, commonly called bow-tie)

1 lb. calamari steak

¼ cup olive oil, divided

4 Tbsp. butter

2 Tbsp. lemon juice

Capers to taste, *optional*

Salt and pepper to taste

1. Cook farfalle according to package instructions. *Any dry pasta noodle may be substituted.*
2. Cut calamari steak into bite size pieces. Heat skillet over moderate heat with half the olive oil and cook calamari until opaque, about 5 minutes.
3. In separate pan, brown the butter, stirring frequently until bubbles dissipate and butter is thoroughly browned. Immediately add remaining olive oil and lemon juice.
4. Toss calamari and capers in butter mixture, salt and pepper to taste.

Eight decades as host and guest at home and away
1993–2002

Through the years, my spirits have been rejuvenated in monastic space, often with repeated visits to Bolton Abbey (Cistercian) in central Ireland, Glasshampton (Franciscan) in England's Midlands, Rostrever (Benedictine) in the Mourne Mountains of Northern Ireland, and St. Gregory's (Episcopal Benedictine) amid the farms of southern Michigan. Nourishing simplicity marks monastic meal times. The abbot's bell signals the meal's beginning. The monks bless the plates served before them then devour food feverishly as they listen, each taking a turn reading aloud from a community-chosen book. The bell rings again, reading stops, a prayer is repeated, and the meal is ended. The rhythm of worship integrated with work moves on.

Twenty-five years after my first culinary academic work at Iowa Mennonite School, I signed up for a six session cooking school with Arletta Lovejoy, who owned the Patchwork Quilt Country Inn in rural Middlebury, Indiana. I have a certificate from the New Orleans School of Cooking. My real culinary diploma treasure is hand-lettered by the teacher:

> *In acknowledgement of the fulfillment of the unique workshop program concerning Belgian food cooking, I, Annie Hubinot hereunder named FARBER Anne-Marie, owner of this special education program certifies that* Willard Roth *was successful in all the tasks he had to do including cleaning the dishes, consequently he receives the* chevalier de l'Essure de cuisine *award with my appreciation.*

That day in Annie's kitchen on the outskirts of Brussels shall ever be one of my most cherished.

2003–2012

Intervening years have provided opportunities, particularly as a Mennonite World Conference communications volunteer, to both give and receive hospitality throughout Western Europe and Africa with a touch of India and Nepal.

Afterword

Food is the heart of the matter.

Cafe Dodici offers a most unlikely touch of Tuscany to diners on the southeast corner of the square in the county seat of Washington, Iowa (where the court house archives my birth certificate). Along with describing her dishes on an artistically-inviting menu, co-owner Lorraine Williams philosophizes on how food matters:

> A good meal should be a spiritually uplifting experience of visiting with friends and family, sharing and enjoying good health and food. Such an experience gives harmony for body and mind, and is the perfect way in which to start changing the world.

> *Food is not matter*
> *but the heart of the matter*
> *the flesh of blood, of rock, of water, of earth and sun.*

> *Food is not a commodity which price can capture*
> *but exacting effort carefully sustained,*
> *the life work of countless beings.*

> *With this cooking I enter the heart of the matter,*
> *I enter the intimate activity which makes dreams materialize.*

> *Cooking is not a mystery;*
> *the more heart we put out,*
> *the more heart we put in.*

> *To bring cooking alive,*
> *we give our life.*

> *Giving our life willingly,*
> *we do not get put out.*

Washing, cutting, cleaning,
exploring new ways to give life to our life.
Not knowing already how and what to do,
practice.

Practice the feeling it out of what is not known
through the warmth and anxiety.

—Lorraine Williams, Cafe Dodici
122 S. Iowa Ave.
Washington, IA 52353

God is the source of my food

Howard Thurman (1899–1981) has a way of putting ordinary thoughts in extraordinary words. His rightful insistence that God is the source of the food we share summarizes the strands I have attempted to weave together in this culinary memoir:

> God is the source of all my life;
> God is the source of my food.

Sometimes I forget that I am utterly dependent upon God for my food. When the farmer plants the seed, and when he cultivates the soil, the miracle of growth takes place. This miracle is an act of sheer grace; I do not cause it, I do not understand it, I cannot explain it—I can only describe it and that inadequately. It does not just happen. It is a part of an order, a way of behaving that is inherent in life itself. Truly, I am dependent upon God for my food.

> The taste of food is not the result of my own effort. How wonderful is the miracle of taste! There is a mysterious interaction between the tongue, my nervous system, and the quality of food itself. How this developed, I do not know; what the secret is, always escapes me. The taste of food floats the whole eating experience and gives to it a dimension of delight that joys the mind and gives to the whole being a sense of gentleness and benevolence.

> How can I say "Thank you" to God for food?
> > By making the eating of food a blessed sacrament.
> > By a self-conscious recognition of the source.

By SHARING my food with the hungry.
By knowing that my food is a gift of which I am merely the trustee.

Here in the quietness, I open my heart and mind to the need of others for food, which act is my salutation to God, the Source of all my life.

—Howard Thurman,
Meditations of the Heart
(Friends United Press, 1976)

I know no more fitting final word for my cookbook than the mealtime prayer I learned at my family table:

God is great; God is good;
Let us thank Him for our food.

It is a prayer in keeping with Solomon's wise words:

Go, eat your bread with enjoyment,
And drink your wine with a merry heart;
For God long ago approved what you do.
—Ecclesiastes 9:7

Willard Roth
Elkhart County, Indiana
Feast of the Transfiguration
August 6, 2015

Index